Facing the future

The Institute for Jewish Policy Research (JPR) is an independent think-tank that informs and influences policy, opinion and decision-making on social, political and cultural issues affecting Jewish life.

JPR programmes of research
- Planning for Jewish communities
- Jewish culture: arts, media and heritage
- Israel: impact, society and identity
- Civil society

Planning for Jewish communities includes surveys and research into the infrastructure of organized Jewish communities, helping them to develop policy recommendations and strategies for change in the welfare, educational and social sectors.

Funders of the Long-term Planning for British Jewry project
The Lord Ashdown Charitable Settlement
The John S. Cohen Foundation
Sue Hammerson OBE
The Lord and Lady Haskel Charitable Foundation
Housing Corporation
Jewish Care
Jewish Chronicle
The Stanley Kalms Foundation
The Joseph Levy Charitable Foundation
The Catherine Lewis Foundation
Nightingale House
Norwood
Felix Posen
United Jewish Israel Appeal
The Charles Wolfson Charitable Trust

Facing the future

The provision of long-term care facilities for older Jewish people in the United Kingdom

Oliver Valins

Institute for Jewish Policy Research

First published in Great Britain in 2002 by
Institute for Jewish Policy Research
79 Wimpole Street
London W1G 9RY

in association with
Profile Books Ltd
58A Hatton Garden
London EC1N 8LX

Copyright © Oliver Valins 2002

The moral right of the author has been asserted.

All rights reserved. Without limiting the rights under copyright reserved above, no part of this publication may be reproduced, stored or introduced into a retrieval system, or transmitted, in any form or by any means (electronic, mechanical, photocopying, recording or otherwise), without the prior written permission of both the copyright owners and the publisher of this book.

Designed and typeset in Garamond by MacGuru
info@macguru.org.uk
Printed in Great Britain by Hobbs the Printers

A CIP catalogue record for this book is available from the British Library.

ISBN 0 901113 29 8

Contents

List of tables and figures ix
Acknowledgements xiii
Note on the author xv
Preface xvii

1 **Introduction** 1
   Structure of the report 5

2 **The historical development of social care** 9
   A brief history of British welfare provision 9
   The Jewish approach to old age 19
   Conclusions 29

3 **The care system in the United Kingdom:**
   formal provision for older people 33
   Demographic projections 34
   Different types of care 40
   New Labour social care legislation and initiatives 48
   Conclusions 59

4 **The Jewish community's care system:**
   formal provision for older people 65
   The current demography of British Jewry 66
   Current provision of services to older people 75
   Conclusions 88

5 **The potential social care marketplace: older Jews living in Leeds** 93
   Leeds Jewry 94
   The Leeds Jewish Community Study 96
   Conclusions 109

6 **Institutional care: choosing a care home** 113
   The process of choosing a care home 114
   Key factors in choosing a care home 121
   Conclusions 130

7 **Institutional care: living in a Jewish voluntary sector care home** 133
   A day in the life of Jewish residential and nursing clients 134
   Institutional life 145
   Conclusions 160

8 **Institutional care: key strategic issues** 165
   Financing services 166
   Provision of places 173
   Human resources 176
   Conclusions 186

9 **Towards the future of formal long-term care services for older Jewish people** 189
   The future of long-term care 190
   Planning for the future 200
   Innovation, communication and information technology 208

The research agenda for the long-term planning
of formal care services 219

Bibliography 225
Index 237

List of tables and figures

Tables

Table 3.1 The changing number of older people in the UK over the last century 35
Table 3.2 Care settings for older people 41
Table 3.3 Number of people in the UK receiving domiciliary care 42
Table 3.4 Preferences for formal and informal care 43
Table 3.5 Provision of sheltered and very sheltered housing units for older people, England, 1997 45
Table 3.6 Number of new dwellings built for older people, England, 1989–97 45
Table 3.7 Number of people in the UK receiving long-term institutional care 47
Table 4.1 Synagogue marriages and deaths according to region, 2000 70
Table 4.2 Projections of Jewish population 75+ 73
Table 4.3 Total housing units of UK Jewish housing associations, 2000 80
Table 4.4 Units for older people held by UK Jewish housing associations, 2000 81
Table 4.5 Number of organizations and homes providing residential and nursing care in the UK Jewish voluntary sector, 2001 81
Table 4.6 Residential and nursing homes in the UK Jewish voluntary sector, 2000 82
Table 4.7 Average age and percentage of female clients in Jewish voluntary sector care homes, 2000 87

Table 5.1 Percentage of the Leeds Jewish population that attends a *seder* meal on Passover 99
Table 5.2 Type of meat bought by Leeds Jews 100
Table 5.3 Medical conditions of Leeds Jews 103
Table 5.4 Ease with which older Leeds Jews can carry out essential tasks 105
Table 8.1 Average weekly fees for private clients in Jewish voluntary sector care homes, 2000 167
Table 8.2 Average weekly fees for private clients in UK care homes (1998) and in private homes in the London borough of Barnet (2001) 168

Figures

Figure 3.1 UK population projections, 2001–61 36
Figure 3.2 UK population projections, 1999–2011 37
Figure 3.3 Total UK population according to status (i.e. children, working-age or pensionable-age individuals), 2001–61 39
Figure 4.1 The changing population of British Jewry, 1850–1995 68
Figure 4.2 Estimated Jewish population of the British Isles, 1995 71
Figure 4.3 Estimated Jewish population of Greater London, 1995 72
Figure 4.4 UK Jewish population projections, 1999–2011 ...74
Figure 4.5 Jewish voluntary sector care homes for older people in Britain, 2001 83
Figure 4.6 Jewish voluntary sector care homes for older people in Greater London, 2001 85
Figure 5.1 Percentage of the Leeds Jewish population with additional (non-state) pension schemes 98

LIST OF TABLES AND FIGURES

Figure 5.2 Religious outlook of Leeds Jews 101
Figure 5.3 Jewish religious practice of Leeds Jews
 (2001 survey) and UK Jewry overall (1995 survey) 101
Figure 5.4 Percentage considering moving to
 sheltered housing or residential care in the next
 ten years, Leeds Jews aged 75+ 108
Figure 6.1 Choices and barriers in obtaining long-term
 care accommodation 115

Acknowledgements

I would like to thank the following individuals who agreed to be interviewed for this report: Celia Aaron; Sheila Altman; Carol Andrews, Heathgrove Lodge; Bella Ansell, former president, Jewish Representative Council of Greater Manchester and Region; Sonia Atkins; Joy Cainer, president, Heathlands Village, Manchester; Marilyn Cantor, Penylan House, Cardiff; Sara Clarke, chief executive, Bnai Brith JBG Housing Association; Julie Cooper, matron/manager, Morris Feinmann Home; Asher Corren, former director, Central Council for Jewish Community Services and Nightingale House; Judith Cotzen, Penylan House, Cardiff; Jerry Coussin; Lena Davis; Peter Elton, chairman, Outreach Community and Residential Services; Boyd Farrar, general manager, Heathlands Village; Michael Galley, chief executive, Manchester Jewish Community Care; Anita Gold; Sandie Huntingdon, Age Resource; Ethel Hyman; Tony Krais; Joan Leifer, director, Glasgow Jewish Housing Association; Malcolm Maddox, chief executive, Newark Lodge, Glasgow; Ricky and Lesley Marcus; Karen Phillips, chief executive, Manchester Jewish Federation; Bradley Reback, owner/manager, Sydmar Lodge; Rabbi Rubin, Giffnock and Newlands Synagogue; Judith Russell; Rasheed Sadeyh-Zadeh, RoseAcres; Ernest Schlesinger; Alan and Norma Schwartz, Cardiff Jewish Help-line; Bill Sheehan, director of nursing, Heathlands Village; John Silverman, chief executive, Westmount Housing Association; Leon Smith, chief executive, Nightingale House; Ita Symons, chief executive, Agudas Israel Housing Association; Jan Vallance, campaign/office manager,

Manchester Jewish Federation; Ethne Waldman, chief executive, Jewish Care Scotland; Raymond Warburton, section head, social care, Department of Health; Rebecca Weinberg, director of services, Manchester Jewish Community Care; West London Synagogue Group; Dianna Wolfson, president, Glasgow Jewish Representative Council; the staff at Stuart Young House, Jewish Care (especially Ian Berkoff, Elaine Grossman, Simon Morris, Adrian Moses and Jenny Weinstein); the social work team at the Manchester Jewish Federation (especially Shoshana Barnett, Mark Cunningham, Joyce Khan, Wayne Perry, Claudine Shapiro and Annette Woolfe).

Thanks also to the many residents, relatives and members of staff of the residential and nursing homes I visited across the UK; to Rabbi Jeremy Rosen for advice on traditional Jewish approaches to old age; to Rebecca Schischa who collected the data on kosher meals-on-wheels and Jewish day centres, as well as information on private care homes in the London borough of Barnet; and to Barry Kosmin, Jacqueline Goldberg and Stanley Waterman for their assistance in designing, planning and producing this report.

Finally, I would like to express my appreciation to the referees of this report: Melvyn Carlowe OBE, voluntary sector consultant and former chief executive of Jewish Care; Asher Corren, former director of the Central Council for Jewish Community Services and Nightingale House; Dr Allen Glicksman, director of research and evaluation planning, Philadelphia Corporation for Aging; Dr Sarah Harper, director, Oxford Institute of Ageing, University of Oxford; and Professor Mark Johnson, professor of diversity in health and social care, Mary Seacole Research Centre, De Montfort University.

Note on the author

Dr Oliver Valins is Research Fellow at the Institute for Jewish Policy Research (JPR). He completed his MA at the University of Edinburgh in 1996, before moving to the Department of Geography, University of Glasgow to study for his Ph.D. His doctoral thesis examined issues of identity and the construction of social and spatial boundaries among strictly Orthodox Jews living in contemporary Britain. The research focused on the strictly Orthodox community in Broughton Park, Manchester, and examined how Jews living there practise their religion within a late twentieth-century urban environment. In 1999 he completed his Ph.D. and took up his research post at JPR.

Dr Valins is the author, along with Barry Kosmin and Jacqueline Goldberg, of *The Future of Jewish Schooling: A Strategic Assessment of a Faith-based Provision of Primary and Secondary School Education*, which examined the strengths and weaknesses of Jewish formal educational services. Dr Valins has also published articles in academic and general journals on strictly Orthodox Judaism and on the geography of religion. His current interests relate to issues of ageing, ethnicity, religion and social care, and how traditional ways of life intersect with the realities of providing services in the twenty-first century.

Preface

In the rapidly changing demographic, economic, social and political climate of the United Kingdom, agencies, organizations and communities urgently need to assess how they provide services for older people. They need to consider how these services can remain viable and be in keeping with the needs and expectations of future generations. *Facing the Future: The Provision of Long-term Care Facilities for Older Jewish People in the United Kingdom* provides, for the first time and in one place, much of the key information, data and analysis that is needed for the UK Jewish community to plan strategically how it cares for its older people, particularly in regard to institutional care. Through the collation and analysis of government and communal data, as well as interviews with key individuals from across the country who both supply and use services, this book provides a foundation text for effective strategic decision-making for the long-term care of older Jews in the United Kingdom.

Services in the Jewish community have, for at least the last century, been provided according to the instincts of local groups and the desires of donors, with little regard to demographic and social service trends. This book offers a unique opportunity for providers to review and co-ordinate their services with the benefit of current thinking and information. It also provides current and potential service users the opportunity to understand the system of care provision for older people, and the challenges and opportunities facing the provision of residential and nursing home care for the Jewish community.

Facing the Future is by far the largest and most detailed examination of the services that are provided for older people by the UK Jewish community. However, its interest extends beyond the Jewish community. In many ways Jews living in Britain are demographic pioneers for the rest of society. Jews tend to live longer, have on average a higher socio-economic status, and make up a greater proportion of older people than the national average. As such, the issues being faced by the Jewish community are likely to be experienced by the rest of society in the next ten to twenty years. In particular, the findings of the report have relevance for other ethnic and religious minority communities whose services are not yet as well-developed and whose age profile is, for the moment, younger than that of the Jewish community. With a long history of investment and support for Jewish social care services, the UK Jewish voluntary sector maintains some of the best facilities in the country as well as standards of the very highest quality. Nevertheless, even here there are major financial and structural problems. Accordingly, the implications for government and other policymakers are even more profound.

This book is the fifth piece of research to be published as part of JPR's project, Long-term Planning for British Jewry. This four-year policy research programme aims to influence the development of policies and priorities for Jewish charities and other voluntary organizations in the twenty-first century. The programme is made up of several projects that slot together to form a comprehensive picture of British Jewry's communal organizations and services. These projects build on one another, feeding into a strategic document that will assist the community in planning its future.

For social planning purposes it was necessary at the outset of the Long-term Planning project to map the parameters of the organized Jewish community. It emerged that the Jewish voluntary sector comprises nearly 2,000 financially independent organizations; thus, the income needed to maintain these organizations had to be substantial. The first piece of published research was commissioned to map systematically for the first time the income and expenditure of these organizations across all their funding streams. The report by Peter Halfpenny and Margaret Reid, *The Financial Resources of the Jewish Voluntary Sector*, estimated the income of the sector from all sources in 1997 at just over £500 million. This is several times the expected proportion of the UK national voluntary sector income. Of the different elements that contribute to the income of the UK Jewish voluntary sector, the largest is social care, accounting for £135 million. A second, related study by Ernest Schlesinger, *Grant-making Trusts in the Jewish Sector*, showed that, in 1997–8, almost £4 million pounds in charitable grants were made to welfare organizations in the Jewish community. This was, however, only fourth on the list of recipients, falling considerably behind the Israel-related, strictly Orthodox and education categories.

The existence of 2,000 Jewish voluntary organizations requires that several thousand members of the Jewish community fill unpaid leadership posts on boards of trustees, take on the burdens of financial office and accept legal and moral responsibility for the running of each organization. JPR commissioned and published a third piece of research by Margaret Harris and Colin Rochester, *Governance in the Jewish Voluntary Sector*. The objective of this qualitative study was to explore the issues and challenges faced by those who currently serve on the boards of Jewish voluntary agencies in Britain, including those directly involved in formal social care provision. Some key challenges for all boards were identified, including the pressure of change in terms of increasing professionalization and the problems of recruiting volunteers and leaders. Five specific challenges emerged for the Jewish voluntary sector: the need for co-operation, the challenge of internal divisions, the need for a sense of collective responsibility, the changing demography of the Jewish population and the problem of resources.

The fourth piece of research, *The Future of Jewish Schooling in the United Kingdom* by Oliver Valins, Barry Kosmin and Jacqueline Goldberg, was published in the summer of 2001. This was a strategic assessment of primary and secondary school education and analysed the strengths and weaknesses of full-time Jewish day schooling from a policy perspective. In particular, it discussed whether Jewish day schools—as an example of faith-based schooling—work, and to what extent they meet the needs of pupils, parents, sponsors, Jewish communities and the wider society. It examined key performance data, including national examination results and OFSTED inspection reports, and noted, for example, how pupils at Jewish day schools achieve results that are up to 50 per cent higher than the national average. The report also included data from in-depth interviews with education providers and parents from across Britain.

Facing the Future is a companion to the education report in that it offers an in-depth examination of services available in the Jewish community. The book provides a strategic assessment of older people's care provision by the organized Jewish community, and details the historical development of social care, demographic changes and the range of services currently being provided. Its particular focus is on institutional care provision within Jewish residential and nursing homes, which account for the lion's share of communal and government funding. It addresses key policy concerns in relation to financing services, provision of places and human resources: issues that have previously only been approached on an *ad hoc* basis and without evidence-based research.

Facing the Future also informs the National Survey of British Jewry, the final piece of research in the Long-term Planning process. This survey takes the form of a postal questionnaire that investigates the needs, expectations and lifestyles of the Jewish public. The first phase of this study focused on the Jewish community in Leeds and elicited responses from 1,500 households. Initial findings from those (non-institutionalized) respondents aged 75 or over are included in this report. The largest component of the National Survey covers London and the South-east, with JPR recently distributing over 20,000 questionnaires to households thought to contain at least one Jewish resident.

In combination, the different pieces of the Long-term Planning project will be used to produce a strategic planning document, a co-ordinated plan for the UK Jewish voluntary sector over the next two decades. Finally, although the overall project (and its different constituent parts) is designed for UK Jewish planners, the model of research it sets out—centred on evidenced-based analysis of the inputs, outputs and processes of the voluntary sector—are of great potential value to Jewish and other minority communities world-wide. For those thinking about the future of their communities, the need for effective strategic planning has never been greater. *Facing the Future* seeks to provide one of the key pieces of this policy-planning jigsaw.

1 Introduction

Britain is ageing. Of its sixty million people, more than one in six are over the age of retirement and this proportion is set to increase. The Jewish community is even older, with almost one-quarter of its population aged 65 or over.[1] The demographic realities of an ageing population represent both opportunities and responsibilities for the Jewish community, as well as for the United Kingdom as a whole. In particular, there are considerable challenges for the future provision of formal care services for older people. An increase in both the actual number of older people in the United Kingdom (especially those who are aged 90 or over, the 'oldest old') and their proportion relative to those of working age has major implications for how services are run and financed. Moreover, partly as a response to demographic changes, but also due to changing societal expectations and a shift in political thinking, successive governments have introduced major legislative changes to the care industry for older people. Indeed, a key policy objective of the current New Labour government is to 'modernize' (further) the welfare system. This means that all formal care services—including those provided by the UK Jewish community—will need to adapt and change, or else face becoming extinct or irrelevant.

At this time of major demographic, social, economic and political change, there is an urgent need for the Jewish community to take stock of its current position, and to consider its future directions. This book is designed to help with this process by providing a detailed picture and analysis of the formal long-term care facilities provided for older Jews by the UK Jewish voluntary sector. It focuses on residential and nursing care home provision because this accounts for the lion's share of the money invested every year by the Jewish community (and across the United Kingdom more widely) and is an area of unique and particular concern. Nevertheless, it should be recognized that the majority of older Jews in Britain needing care receive these services outside of institutional settings. This book provides broad indicators of Jewish domiciliary care and day centre services, although specialist research into this area is beyond its scope. Dedicated research on these subjects would be an extremely useful addition to this study.

Overall, the book's aims are:

- to review the current systems of formal social care provision for older Jews living in the United Kingdom;
- to detail key strategic issues faced by institutional care home providers;
- to investigate the needs and wants of older people; and
- to consider future directions for the sector and how services for older people can be improved and developed.

Along the way it surveys the historical development of care provision, presents key demographic changes facing the community, explains how care services operate, and suggests innovative ways in which formal provision for older people may be better co-ordinated and be more in keeping with the needs and wants of users and their families. However, at the outset, it is important to define the way that this report understands old age and older people, so that, in particular, 'they' are not seen as a problem or an inevitable burden on society.

INTRODUCTION

> Inherent in much of the political language used in respect of old age are a number of underlying assumptions which lead to the notion that old age—and the care of those that have finished their working lives and who may have changing needs as their health changes—is somehow a 'problem'. People see it as a 'problem' that society is somehow managing to contain at the moment ... In this age of opportunity, while physical capabilities or mental faculties may change, people should not necessarily be assumed to be passive recipients of the goodwill of others or inevitably incapacitated, befuddled or redundant. Society should recognise the value inherent in older people, and the value to society in using ingenuity to help people to continue to realise their potential more effectively.[2]

Most older people continue to live in their own homes and do not require formalized long-term care. Being old can be immensely liberating, and the political and economic power of older people—so called 'grey power' and the 'grey pound'—has never been greater. Prevailing attitudes towards older people based on physical appearance or incapacity are potentially as damaging and discriminatory as negative stereotypes based on people's race, gender or class. But, by the same measure, it is equally important not to be naive about or to downplay the very real problems and issues faced by many older people, a misunderstanding that is potentially just as damaging. For those who are physically and mentally frail, there may be very real problems and challenges, ranging from difficulties shopping or using public transport to coping with progressive forms of dementia. Nevertheless, there is great potential and value in younger people examining their attitudes to old age, and it is in this spirit that this study should be read.

The book has been written for both providers and users of services for older Jewish people living in the United Kingdom. The aim is to provide a comprehensive picture of the range of services provided, and the strengths, weaknesses and key strategic issues facing institutional care providers. Community planning of social care services for older people requires an assessment of a complex set of criteria to determine likely future needs and the ability of the community to provide the type and the range of services expected. Planning involves piecing together a jigsaw of different elements, such as the history of the way in which care has traditionally been provided, demographic changes both in the Jewish community and throughout the United Kingdom, the impact of government legislation and initiatives, current levels of service provision, the future needs and expectations of clients, and key strategic issues and barriers that threaten (or indeed provide opportunities for) improvements and modernization. Only by viewing the *whole picture* can effective strategic planning be carried out, enabling the community—as *the* key stakeholders in any decisions made—to realize what can and cannot be achieved.

Facing the Future is an analysis based on a wide range of government and community data sources. These include demographic trends from the Government Actuary Department (GAD) and the Community Research Unit of the Board of Deputies, as well as a telephone survey of all the Jewish organizations across the United Kingdom that provide meals-on-wheels, day centre services, sheltered housing, and residential and nursing home care. Interviews were also conducted with service providers across the country, including care home managers, chief executives of housing associations, social workers and community professionals. Service users were also interviewed, including individuals with relatives in care homes and older people themselves. An analysis is also included of the results of a postal survey of the Leeds Jewish community carried out in August 2000, which represented 1,500 respondents in Jewish households across the city. Responses of those aged 75 or over are included in Chapter 5, which examines the potential market for social care services.

Structure of the book

The book is designed to provide the various informational and analytical jigsaw pieces needed for effective strategic planning. Chapter 2 begins this process by detailing the historical development of social care. It examines traditional care provision in Britain, in the Jewish community over time, and that supplied more particularly by Jews living in this country. The current systems of care strongly bear the imprints of their respective historical developments, and understanding these is important for future planning. Chapters 3 and 4 detail the systems of formal care services provided for older people in the United Kingdom and by the Jewish community. These chapters outline demographic projections, details of the range of care services that are currently being provided, and the impact of current and forthcoming government legislation and initiatives on the sector. Chapter 5 introduces initial findings from the JPR Leeds Community Survey, providing a detailed quantitative profile of the lifestyles and characteristics of those Jews aged 75 or over who are either current or potential users of formal social care services. The older Leeds Jewish community is compared to that in the United Kingdom as a whole, indicating some key differences in the health and mobility characteristics of these populations.

Chapters 6, 7 and 8 explicitly concentrate on institutional care provision. While most older people remain independent—and any long-term services they do use are likely to take the form of domiciliary assistance or care within day centres—residential and nursing homes are by far the most expensive form of provision within the Jewish community (as indeed they are across Britain more widely). As such, it is appropriate to examine these services in more depth. Chapter 6 looks at the processes by which people choose a care home for themselves or (increasingly) for close relatives. Chapter 7 provides an insight into the everyday realities of life inside Jewish long-term care institutions. It does this through three day-in-the-life case-studies of residents in Jewish institutions: a residential client, a person in an elderly mentally infirm (EMI) unit and a nursing home client. These case-studies provide markers according to which the strengths and weaknesses of current forms of provision, and some of the challenges facing providers seeking to improve and develop their services, can be understood. Chapter 8 outlines some of the key strategic issues facing Jewish institutional providers, including issues relating to financing services, calculating the likely future demand for places, as well as to the challenges of human resources given national staffing shortages and a lack of Jewish staff. Finally, Chapter 9 draws together all the previous data and analyses and considers future directions in the provision of services to older Jews in the United Kingdom. It discusses innovative ways in which the current system can be developed and rethought, including the improvement of connections between different Jewish social care organizations, the use of 'assistive technology', the development of the use of information technology, and the rethinking of some of the fundamentals that shape the way that care has traditionally been provided.

Notes

1 Marlena Schmool and Frances Cohen, *A Profile of British Jewry: Patterns and Trends at the Turn of a Century* (London: Board of Deputies of British Jews 1998).
2 Royal Commission on Long Term Care, *With Respect to Old Age: Long Term Care—Rights and Responsibilities* (London: Stationery Office 1999), 3–4.

2 The historical development of social care

The first step towards effective strategic planning is an understanding of the historical development of social care services. The first part of this chapter provides a brief history of British welfare provision, detailing the changing ways in which society has dealt with those who are poor, needy, elderly or infirm. The shift in attitudes to welfare and the delivery of care can be seen in the transition from the relative harshness of the workhouse (designed to provide living conditions that would be a deterrent to those seeking to use its facilities) to the introduction of the Welfare State in the 1940s. More recently there has been a spate of reforms that have aimed to de-institutionalize care services so as to promote people's independence and reduce costs to the taxpayer. The second part of the chapter looks at the Jewish approach to old age, examining the foundations of the Jewish system of care from biblical times to the present. Jews have a very long history of caring for those in need, which is reflected in the range of services currently provided. Nevertheless, the history of care provision in the Jewish community also strongly reflects the influences of wider societal norms and expectations.

A brief history of British welfare provision

Little is known about the provision of formal welfare services in the United Kingdom before the late Middle Ages, but by mediaeval times the church had become central to the establishment of formal philanthropy through the dispensation of alms and care for the poor. Priests and monks were legally bound to expend their revenue (partly derived from tithes) in furnishing almshouses and providing elementary education for the poor. By the fifteenth century the role of the church was beginning to decline, and there was increasing dissatisfaction with the running of ecclesiastical institutions. At the same time, feudal landlords developed a paternalistic attitude to the well-being of their tenants, although this inevitably varied from case to case. From the fourteenth century, guilds and livery companies also emerged. These were primarily established to protect trade, but they also established primitive forms of social insurance and contributed to the maintenance of almshouses and the support of local paupers. However, these ceased to play a role in welfare provision by the end of the sixteenth century, although the London livery companies remain major philanthropic institutions to the present day.[1]

In the seventeenth century a much enlarged social elite composed of the gentry, the urban aristocracy and merchants took on a greater role in welfare provision. Almshouses, hospitals, houses of correction, workhouses, work programmes, apprentice schemes, grammar schools and universities all benefitted from a new era of benevolence. At the same time, the role of the state also expanded as the number of landless poor increased: 'detached from the customary support of Tudor feudal society—and with the monastic network no longer in place to provide support—the landless poor now appeared to the elite to be posing a major threat to social order and stability.'[2] In response, the Tudor state developed an increasingly sophisticated Poor Law through the (in)famous 1601 Statute on Charitable Uses. This statute formalized a division of the poor into the employable and the unemployable. The former, characterized as the 'undeserving poor', were the responsibility of local parishes, which could provide relief or (increasingly) the deterrent of the workhouse. The latter, the 'deserving poor', were to be supported by private philanthropy, with donors supposedly secure in the knowledge that they were aiding the worthy disadvantaged, rather than the merely 'idle'. By the first half of the eighteenth century this had given way to a more tolerant attitude towards welfare provision, although this changed again by the end of the century and the advent of the industrial revolution.

By the start of the nineteenth century, the growing urbanization of society, major fears of insurrection and social disorder following the French Revolution, as well as a concern with over-population, led to an increasing harshness and moralization in the philosophy of welfare. The reform of the Poor Law in 1834 had deterrence as its central tenet, so that poor relief and, in particular, life in the workhouse were to be made less attractive than the situation of the poorest labourers.[3] Dependency on the state was to be avoided as far as possible. Despite the harshness of the Poor Law, the same period also witnessed developments in working-class organizations, especially friendly societies and trade clubs, which by the end of the century had evolved into trade unions. Soup kitchens, hospitals, medical dispensaries and institutions for training disabled people were also established. Even so:

> There is strong evidence that the Victorian poor were
> not content with their lot. Contemporary reports suggest
> irritation with the moralising cant of the relief workers,
> and resentment at providing a hobby for the Evangelical
> middle-class whose women were precluded by custom
> from gainful employment.[4]

Many commentators view the second half of the nineteenth century as the heyday of British philanthropy, with middle-class families spending much of their income on charity (apparently only second to their outlay on food). There were even criticisms about services being duplicated, with some families besieged by different individuals and welfare agencies seeking to support them. Others, however, living in less fortuitous geographical locations, were bypassed completely.[5]

The turn of the twentieth century witnessed an increasing role for the state in welfare provision. The rise of the Labour Party, the realization of the poor medical condition of recruits for the Boer War in South Africa and in the First World War, as well as the era of depression that followed that war, led to the state taking an increasingly active role in welfare provision. The political climate was such that, if Britain were to be economically and militarily successful and to compete with foreign powers, the state would have to be more proactive in maintaining the health of its individual citizens.

The 1940s marked the greatest change in the balance between state and voluntary provision of welfare, most notably with the creation of the Welfare State by the post-Second World War Labour government. The combined effects of the Education Act 1944, the National Health Service Act 1946, the National Insurance Act 1946 and the National Assistance Act 1948 were to relegate the voluntary sector to 'junior partner' in the provision of welfare and educational services. Indeed, some in the Labour Party hoped that state-sector provision would put an end to the voluntary sector, with its associations of middle-class paternalism and the maintenance of class divisions. The welfare and educational needs of the population were to be provided free to all at the point of demand, regardless of social or economic status, 'from cradle to grave'.[6]

By the 1970s practical and ideological limitations of the Welfare State were becoming increasingly evident, although the important 1978 Wolfenden Committee report, *The Future of Voluntary Organisations*, foresaw few of the radical changes that were shortly to shake the sector.[7] In the 1980s and 1990s Conservative governments sought to redefine radically the role of the state *vis-à-vis* the private and public sectors. Nationalized industries such as electricity, gas, telecommunications and the railways were privatized, as the government sought to reduce public service spending and deliver tax cuts. The voluntary sector, characterized as the junior partner in the delivery of welfare services since the 1940s, was to become more prominent. The dual aims were to increase consumer choice—at least for those with suitable financial savings—and to ease the burden on the public purse. The (New) Labour government under Tony Blair has largely adopted these aims, and has sought to end traditional Labour distrust of the private and voluntary sectors (through its Third Way politics) and to promote the use of 'non-state actors' in the delivery of formal care services. At the 2001 general election it also promised a vast increase in spending on public services, although this is to be targeted in specific areas, especially education and the National Health Service (NHS). In terms of social care for older people, recent years have witnessed major regulatory changes and a raft of initiatives. Unfortunately, government acceptance of the financial implications of these changes for service providers has been much slower.

Care for older people

The history of formal care for older people in the United Kingdom closely parallels that of welfare provision more generally. In mediaeval times, monasteries and convents provided institutional care, while almshouses were also widely established. The Poor Law Act of 1601 required the local parish to provide for elderly paupers, and by the nineteenth century the (dreaded) public workhouse was providing much of the 'care' to those older people without alternative means. In 1909 the Royal Commission on the Poor Laws reported that some 140,000 older people were resident in Poor Law institutions. This, combined with the hugely influential reports on poverty by Booth in 1899 and Rowntree in 1910, helped foster a climate of reform in institutional care, as well as subtle, but important, changes in public perceptions about the place of older people in society.[8] The 1908 Old Age Pensions Act was an initial step in this direction, although it was not until the 1940s that the relationship between older people and the workhouse was more directly tackled.

In an attempt to remove the stigma of the workhouse, the 1948 National Assistance Act stipulated that elderly residents needing institutional care were to be charged a modest fee. While the fee was reimbursed from the old age pension, the aim was to change the ethos of these institutions from one of 'inmate' and 'master', to that of a 'hotel'-style environment. Institutions were to be built on a smaller scale, with the Minister of Health, Aneurin Bevan, arguing in 1947 that the optimum limit was 25–30 persons.

> The old institutions or workhouses are to go altogether. In their place will be attractive hostels or hotels, each accommodating 25 to 30 people, who will live there as guests not inmates. Each guest will pay for his accommodation—those with private income out of that, those without private income out of the payments they get from the National Assistance Board—and nobody

need know whether they have private means or not. Thus, the stigma of 'relief'—very real too, and acutely felt by many old people—will vanish at last.[9]

Despite the optimism, the reality of institutional care proved somewhat different. A shortage of building materials in the 1950s and fears about the ageing of the population led to the limit of 25–30 residents being revised upwards, with a figure of 60 being suggested by the Ministry of Health in 1954. There were arguments concerning the distinction between hospital and social care, and the original system also took a tough line on savings and capital investment: the committee established to examine the break up of the Poor Law, headed by Sir Arthur Rucker, concluded that it was perfectly reasonable for those entering institutional care to put any capital they had (including their house) towards their long-term care.[10] Moreover, according to the social commentator Peter Townsend, there was a lack of planning in the development of care and a failure to ask older people themselves what they really wanted:

> The blunt fact is that the government has tried to abandon the policies of the Poor Law without sufficiently considering the alternative policies that should take their place. It is no less astonishing that in the middle of the twentieth century new policies can be introduced and after a decent interval modified, without detailed inquiry into both the best use of existing buildings and the needs and wishes of persons living there.[11]

The 1948 Act gave local authorities powers to support residents in private and voluntary sector homes, but the number of these institutions remained relatively small, with few new facilities being constructed until the 1960s. Moreover, much of the existing accommodation was of a poor standard, with little actual change from the Victorian institutions that had been so condemned in the Rowntree report.

> Much of this elderly accommodation had further deteriorated, multi-occupancy of rooms was the norm, and basic amenities such as hand-basins, toilets and baths were not only insufficient but were often difficult to reach, badly distributed and of poor quality. Ministry of Health reports were admitting that 'local authorities have been reluctant to incur expenditure on old premises that they hoped soon to relinquish'. Other research highlighted that many of the converted homes were completely unsuited for use as residential homes because of their geographical isolation and poor access standards.[12]

The staffing situation was little better: 'a minority of them were unsuitable, by any standards, for the tasks they performed, men or women with authoritarian attitudes inherited from Poor Law days who provoked resentment or even terror among infirm people'.[13] During the 1960s regulations were introduced for care homes in the private and voluntary sectors, and the Ministry of Housing also began the development of sheltered housing initiatives within the public sector. This formed part of a wider package of government subsidies towards social housing, which saw a rapid increase in stock managed by registered social landlords. At the same time, the Ministry of Health also sought to develop 'community care' so that services could be provided to people in their own homes, rather than in institutions.

With the election of the Thatcher government in 1979, the 'market' for the institutional care of older people was opened up. One of the most dramatic results of this was a shift in the balance between the proportion of private care homes and those in the public sector. In 1976 there was a ratio of one person in a private residential home for every five in public sector homes; by 1982 the ratio was one to three; in 1989 it was one to one; and in 1992 there were two people resident in private homes for every one in the public sector. Much of this increase was due to cuts in spending by local authorities on their own homes, combined with the availability of relatively generous, means-tested cash payments from central government to older people requiring residential or nursing care. These payments acted as *de facto* vouchers. Depending on their financial situation, older people would be funded to live in care homes, regardless of whether this form of care was really the most appropriate.[14]

During the 1990s the Conservative government under John Major introduced specific legislation to reform long-term care for older people through the 1990 National Health Service and Community Act. This act had a number of key intentions:

- Encourage an alteration in the balance of care from institutional to community care, discouraging long-term hospital provision and residential and nursing home placements;
- Engineer a move from supply-led towards needs-led decisions and service arrangements;
- Enhance the role of both the private and voluntary sectors through the deployment of contractual and quasi-contractual agreements, and through the creation of 'not-for-profit' providers to manage

floated off services formerly directly run by local authorities; and
- Move much more responsibility for community care decision making and funding to local authorities, and away from central government (the National Health Service and Department of Social Security).[15]

Included within these changes was an emphasis on 'choice', under which local authorities were legally required to allow older people to choose their own care home, although within certain limitations of cost and suitability. The changes implemented under the 1990 Act were in keeping with Conservative enthusiasm for markets and consumer-led services, a desire to de-institutionalize care by providing services in people's own homes wherever possible, transferring the blame for apparent under-funding and service failures from central to local government, and minimizing public spending to enable tax cuts.[16] Nevertheless, these changes failed to halt the inexorable increase in government spending on long-term care or, indeed, to solve key fundamental problems in the funding system overall. These problems were recognized by the New Labour government of Tony Blair, which came to power in a landslide victory in May 1997. To address problems on the future funding of long-term care, the Secretary of State for Health, Frank Dobson, established a royal commission. Its remit was:

> To examine the short and long term options for a sustainable system of funding Long Term Care for elderly people, both in their own homes and in other settings, and ... to recommend how, and in what circumstances, the cost of such care should be apportioned between public funds and individuals.[17]

The Commission made several recommendations, including that all personal care in residential and nursing homes should be paid for from general taxation and not from fees charged to residents. The government accepted only in part the Commission's recommendations, leaving a system that is still deeply problematic and with severe funding problems. These issues, together with the impact of other major government initiatives—for example the *National Service Framework for Older People*, the *NHS Plan*, the *Better Care, Higher Standards* charter for long-term care, the *Supporting People* framework for support services, and the Care Standards 2000 Act that is introducing national minimum standards for care services—are examined in Chapter 3.[18]

The Jewish approach to old age

> If there be among you a needy man, one of your brethren, within thy gate, in thy land which the Lord thy God giveth thee, thou shalt not harden thy heart nor shut thy hand from thy needy brother; but thou shalt surely open thy hand unto him and shalt surely lend him sufficient for his need in that which he wanteth.[19]

According to Jewish tradition and *halakhah* (Jewish law), charity is considered one of the cardinal *mitzvot* (good deeds) of Judaism. According to the talmudic text *Ethics of the Fathers*, the practice of charity is, along with Torah and service (i.e. prayer), one of the pillars upon which the world rests.[20] The Hebrew word most often used to describe charity is *zedakah*, although this literally means 'righteousness' or 'justice': hence, charity is not to be seen as a favour to the poor, but rather something to which they have a right, and donors an obligation. Everyone is obliged to give to charity; even people who are dependent on charity should donate to those less fortunate. To give a tenth of one's wealth is considered a 'middling' virtue, a twentieth 'mean', although one shouldn't give more than a fifth as this may lead to the impoverishment of the donor. In biblical times, the courts could compel people to pay their fair share of charity, with those who refused liable to flogging and to having their property appropriated.[21] In the thirteenth century, a group of pietistic Jews in Germany (known as the Saints of Germany) argued that God would punish the rich as if they had robbed from the poor: hence, the advocacy of a redistribution of wealth according to divine rules of social equality and justice.[22]

The mediaeval Jewish philosopher and talmudist Maimonides listed eight progressively virtuous ways of giving *zedakah*:

> to give but sadly; less than is fitting, but in good
> humour; only after having been asked to; before being
> asked; in such a manner that the donor does not know
> who the recipient is; in such a manner that the recipient
> does not know who the donor is; and in such a way
> that neither the donor nor the recipient knows the
> identity of the other.

However, the highest form of charity is not to give alms, but rather to help the poor rehabilitate themselves, for example by lending them money, taking them into partnership or else giving them work.[23] In talmudic sources, the primary unit of charity and social support is considered to be the family. Where family support is unavailable, the second unit of support is the community. The Torah also expects Jews to be aware of the needs of the stranger, because Israelites were themselves strangers in the land of Egypt.

> Charity should be dispensed to the non-Jewish poor in order to preserve good relations; however charity should not be accepted from them unless it is entirely unavoidable. Women take precedence over men in receiving alms, and one's poor relatives come before strangers. The general rule is 'the poor of your own town come before the poor of any other town,' but this rule is lifted for the poor of *Erez Israel* [the land of Israel] who take precedence over all.[24]

With regard to older people, the Torah characterizes barbaric enemy states as those 'who will show the old no regard'.[25] In ancient Israel older people were highly respected and were accorded a central place in the family and the tribal structure. Old age in the Torah is associated with wisdom and knowledge—indeed the term 'elders' is used as a synonym for judges, leaders and sages—and is connected to the exhortation to fear, honour and obey one's parents. Indeed, it is a biblical obligation for children to look after their parents—the fifth commandment is to honour them—and the courts in talmudic times could compel people to do so.[26] Praise from the Talmud for older people includes the following advice: 'if the old say "tear down" and the young "build"—tear down, for the "destruction" of the old is construction; the "construction" of the young, destruction'.[27] At the same, the Talmud recognizes that with old age may come a loss of intellectual and physical capacities; the very old were forbidden to serve as members of the *Sanhedrin* (legal court of the Temple).[28] The Talmud also identifies the difficulties older people face in continuing to earn a living.[29]

Nevertheless, despite the range of references to older people in biblical and talmudic literature, there are no specific regulations (and indeed no attempt to create designated institutions) for caring for older people:

> If not living among the family, as was customary, destitute aged people were treated as part of the general social problem created by poverty and weakness and precepts concerning charity and alms giving (*zedakah*) applied to them. Thus, although old age was originally invested with strength and majesty, people of the lower strata who had lost the support and care provided by the family underwent much suffering, if not humiliation, in their old age.[30]

In mediaeval times, Jews became increasingly concentrated in towns and, being in environments that were often hostile and antisemitic, Jewish feelings of solidarity increased. Charitable associations developed that were known as *hevrot* or brotherhoods. Individual *hevrot* dowered poor brides, saw to the needs of the sick and took care of older people and itinerants. The most prestigious of the groups was the *hevra kadisha* (literally 'holy brotherhood'), which was responsible for burying the dead and was also typically a major philanthropic agency in its own right.

> There were no professionals, and in a sense no volunteers as we now know them. The opportunity to participate in a brotherhood was not open to all ... To become a member you were vetted by those already recognized by the community as persons of probity, piety and—in some instances—wealth. To serve in a brotherhood was an honour bestowed rather than a position sought.[31]

Local sick people were, as in talmudic times, cared for in their own homes and were dependent on the resources of their immediate family. Transients and those without family support were, however, cared for in the *hekdesh*, a communal shelter and infirmary that varied in size from a single rented room to a group of small buildings, typically located outside of the town near the cemetery. Local inhabitants generally regarded the *hekdesh* with horror because of its unsanitary conditions. Even as late as the nineteenth century, a British missionary visiting the Jewish hospital in Minsk (which developed from the old *hekdesh*) noted its unsanitary conditions:

> In the Jewish hospital we saw 45 young and old of both sexes, seemingly without the classification of disease, placed in several rooms. They certainly presented one of the most appalling scenes of wretchedness I ever witnessed; filth, rags and pestilential effluvia pervaded the whole place.[32]

Until their near destruction during the Second World War, a large proportion of the world's Jews lived in small, semi-rural towns in Eastern Europe known as *shtetls*. In these towns, Jews practised their religion, formed close communities, spoke in the distinctive language of Yiddish, and bargained with the local population in the latter's language, whether Polish, Hungarian or Ukrainian. Within these communities, older people were an integral and valued part of society, with the importance of kinship—and links between children, parents and grandparents—a key legacy for contemporary Jewish life.[33]

> No matter how old a person is when his wife or husband dies, he is not too old to marry. It is not

> merely that man should not be alone. Age is not necessarily equated with decline nor is it considered in itself a reason for retirement. In all areas a person expects and strives to be an active participant as long as he lives. Life is seen as a path of expanding gratification. The older one is, the more mature he is, the more ripe, the better as a human being. Aged couples expect to enjoy as well as to help each other. Age is good. Old people are 'beautiful'. If a man of eighty marries a woman of seventy-five, they expect it to be a good marriage in every sense of the word.[34]

Despite the attributes of old age, there were major social pressures and expectations that created difficulties for children looking after parents who were no longer able to support themselves. Older men in particular considered it a wound to their self-esteem to be supported by their children: 'better to beg one's bread from door to door than to be dependent on one's son'.[35] Indeed, some men apparently preferred to move to a home for the aged, supported by impersonal funds, rather than be dependent on their own children: 'the dignity of old age can better endure the impersonal than the personal benefaction'.[36]

Another important component of Jewish life is family death rituals. The defining 'vital' moments in the lives of Jewish people are marked by ritual events, including the circumcision of male babies, *bar* and *bat mitzvah* ceremonies to mark the passage into adulthood, marriage, and death itself. When a person dies, the burial usually takes place as soon as possible afterwards, and a series of ritual and religious events traditionally take place to mark their passing and to mourn for them. For the week following the burial, surviving parents, the spouse, siblings and children of the deceased mourn at home (sit *shivah*), where prayer services are held. For the following eleven months, a special prayer (the mourner's *kaddish*) is said by close relatives, and before the end of this period there is a stone-setting ceremony at which the tombstone is consecrated. On the anniversary of a person's death (*yahrzeit* in Yiddish) it is customary to light a twenty-four-hour candle and to recite *kaddish*. On the last day of Passover, during the festivals of Shavuot and Shemini Azeret, and on Yom Kippur (Day of Atonement), memorial (*yizkor*) prayers are said for the departed. These events are key ways in which individuals come to terms with their grief, but they are also important in reaffirming attachments to the community and maintaining Jewish identity.

Jewish welfare provision in the United Kingdom

Following their exile by Edward I in 1290, Oliver Cromwell permitted Jews to return to England in 1656 only on condition that they would not become a burden on the state and would take responsibility for their poor. While church and state were happy to avoid a drain on their finances, it also suited Jews to maintain a separate welfare system in keeping with their particular religious and cultural needs, most obviously the requirements of having kosher food and observing the Sabbath. As a network of Jewish welfare organizations developed during Victorian times, this autonomy was maintained. These organizations typically mirrored those of the wider British voluntary sector, although the Poor Law, and in particular the provisions of the workhouse, were largely side-stepped by British Jewish communities, who sought to provide for their own. Welfare provision was largely organized through the synagogues, but throughout the eighteenth and nineteenth centuries a range of other Jewish voluntary organizations developed. For example, in London there was the Bread and Coals Society, the Sabbath Meals Society and the Soup Kitchen for the Jewish Poor. There were also a series of bricks-and-mortar institutions, including the Home and Hospital for Jewish Incurables built in 1889, the Hand-in-Hand Asylum for Aged and 'Decayed' Tradesmen, the Joel Emanuel almshouses, the Spanish and Portuguese Hospital, the Ashkenazi Jews' Hospital, and Nightingale House (Home for Aged Jews, established in 1840 in the East End of London, before moving to its present site in Clapham, South London in 1900).[37]

Despite the proliferation of organizations in the eighteenth and nineteenth centuries, there were problems co-ordinating services. An attempt to create a Jewish Poor Board for London collapsed because the Act of Parliament required for this was defeated. There were further attempts in 1841 and 1844, but it was only in 1859 that representatives of the three major synagogues in the City of London—the Great, the New and Hambro's—combined their relief services to form the Board of Guardians for the Relief of the Jewish Poor.[38] The London Board of Guardians was the largest in the United Kingdom, but each major Jewish centre had such an organization, the oldest of which was founded in Liverpool.

During the first half of the twentieth century, there was a gradual change in the emphasis of Jewish voluntary organizations from relief to welfare, with statutory services increasingly taking over the role of communal charities. This was further enhanced with the Labour government's introduction of the Welfare State in the 1940s.

> In some respects the introduction of the Welfare State from 1948 onwards was another 'golden age' which helped encourage a very thriving voluntary sector. For members of the Jewish community, long used to

providing volunteers and volunteer services, it meant
that a combination of their manpower and financial
resources with government support helped form
services which in many instances were innovations of
their kind and the envy of the social services world.[39]

Nevertheless, with the decline of the supposedly all-encompassing nature of the Welfare State from the 1970s, Jewish voluntary organizations had to take an increasingly active role in the direct provision of, and financial support for, the welfare needs of the community. In 1972 the Jewish Welfare Board (formerly the Jewish Board of Guardians), the Jewish Blind Society, Norwood Child Care and the Jewish Home and Hospital at Tottenham set up the Central Council for Jewish Social Services. The aim of the Council was to co-ordinate social services so that provision could be better planned and duplication avoided, similar to the American Jewish community model. Because of a lack of financial clout, however, the Council never really achieved its aims, although it did become an important forum for debate and the exchange of views.

In 1990 the Jewish Welfare Board and the Jewish Blind Society merged to form Jewish Care. Jewish Care has since expanded to incorporate the Jewish Home and Hospital at Tottenham, Food for the Jewish Poor (Soup Kitchen), the Jewish Association for the Physically Handicapped, British Tay-Sachs Foundation, Waverly Manor, Brighton and Hove Jewish Home, Stepney (Bnai Brith) Clubs and Settlement, Sinclair House and, most recently, the Otto Schiff Housing Association (OSHA). Jewish Care is the biggest Jewish social service provider in the United Kingdom. With the rise of Jewish Care, the need for the Central Council was seen to have declined; this, together with a variety of internal factors, brought the Council's operations effectively to an end by the close of the 1990s.

The combination of different service providers under the mantle of Jewish Care represented a considered and co-ordinated attempt by community leaders to create a one-stop, unified approach to welfare delivery for the South-east of England. However, it also reflects the problems that many middle-sized organizations have in surviving as independent agencies and institutions in the climate of the modern Welfare State.

> ... in response to the Treasury's ever-increasing demands that more of the burden of responsibility is thrust back on to the shoulders of the community rather than on the Exchequer ... once again, the British Jewish Community is having to face up to the challenge of underpinning its comprehensive network of social services. Now, almost a century after the heyday of Victorian Jewish social welfare provision, British Jewry is once again being asked to look after its own, primarily utilising its own resources and energy.[40]

At present, the UK Jewish voluntary sector consists of almost 2,000 financially independent organizations (3,700 if subsidiary organizations and branches are included), ranging from multi-million pound agencies, such as Jewish Care, to small family-run charities and grant-making trusts.[41] Each city with a sizeable Jewish population has its own charitable organizations, including community care facilities (developed from the old welfare boards and boards of guardians) and institutional care homes. This extensive, but sometimes disparate, network provides care to thousands of Jewish people every week.

Conclusions

The provision for needy people, and for those who are older in particular, has changed and evolved over the centuries. In Britain this has swung from the harshness of the Poor Law days, to the relative benevolence of the 1940s and the Welfare State, to the current climate of reform, modernization and a desire to cap expenditure. Jews living in the United Kingdom and elsewhere in the world have a long tradition of caring for members of the community who are in need; indeed charity is one the fundamental pillars on which Judaism rests. Older people have also traditionally been seen as valued members of communities and an integral part of family life. Nevertheless, the services provided for older Jewish people have also been strongly influenced by the prevailing political, social and economic climate. As such, with successive governments seeking to 'roll back' the state from service provision, the community is faced with ever-greater demands to care for those most in need. The capital sums for buildings and infrastructure have, since the beginnings of the UK Jewish voluntary sector, almost always come from community sources rather than from the state. In today's social care environment, however, the (financial and social) burden on the Jewish community to provide day-to-day service provision is—without significant changes in government policy—likely to be ever greater.

Notes

1 Jeremy Kendall and Martin Knapp, *The Voluntary Sector in the UK* (Manchester: Manchester University Press 1996).
2 Ibid., 32.

3   Pat Thane, *Old Age in English History: Past Experiences, Present Issues* (Oxford: Oxford University Press 2000); Peter Townsend, *The Last Refuge* (London: Routledge and Kegan Paul 1962).
4   Ian Williams, quoted in Kendall and Knapp, 39.
5   Ibid.
6   Ibid.
7   John Wolfenden, *The Future of Voluntary Organisations* (London: Croom Helm 1978).
8   Sheila M. Peace, Leonie Kellaher and Dianne Willcocks, *Re-evaluating Residential Care* (Buckingham: Open University Press 1997).
9   R. Garland, quoted in Robin Means, 'Lessons from the history of long-term care for older people', in Janice Robinson (ed.), *Towards a New Social Compact for Care in Old Age* (London: King's Fund 2001), 9–27 (16). See also Robin Means and Randall Smith, *From Poor Law to Community Law: The Development of Welfare Services for Elderly People 1939–1971* (Bristol: Policy Press 1998), and Thane.
10 Means, 'Lessons from the history'.
11 Townsend, *Last Refuge*, 39.
12 Means, 'Lessons from the history', 16.
13 Peter Townsend, quoted in ibid., 17.
14 Jeremy Kendall, *The Third Sector and Social Care for Older People in England: Towards an Explanation of Its Contrasting Contributions in Residential Care, Domiciliary Care and Day Care*, Civil Society Working Paper 8 (London: Personal Social Services Research Unit (PSSRU), London School of Economics 2000).
15 Ibid., 8.
16 Ibid.; see also Peace *et al.*
17 Royal Commission on Long Term Care, ix.
18 Department of Health, *National Service Framework for Older People* (London: Department of Health Publications 2001); Department of Health, *The NHS Plan: A Plan for Investment; A*

Plan for Reform, Cm 4818-I (London: Stationery Office 2000); Department of Health/Department of the Environment, Transport and the Regions, *Better Care, Higher Standards: A Charter for Long Term Care* (London: Department of Health Publications 2001); Department of the Environment, Transport and the Regions, *Supporting People: Policy into Practice* (London: Department of the Environment, Transport and the Regions 2001); Department of Health, *Care Homes for Older People: National Minimum Standards* (London: Stationery Office 2001).

19 Deuteronomy 15: 7–8.
20 Pirkei Avot 1: 2.
21 Gittin 7a; Ketubah 49b.
22 *Encyclopaedia Judaica*, 16 vols (Jerusalem: Keter 1971–2), v.345.
23 Ibid., v.343.
24 Shulchan Aruch Yoreh Deah, in ibid., v.341.
25 Deuteronomy 28: 50.
26 Kiddushin 29a.
27 Megillah 31b.
28 Sanhedrin 36b.
29 Kiddushin 82b.
30 *Encyclopaedia Judaica*, ii.343.
31 Barry Kosmin, 'Foreword', in Margaret Harris, *The Jewish Voluntary Sector in the United Kingdom: Its Role and Its Future* (London: Institute for Jewish Policy Research 1997), 1.
32 *Encyclopaedia Judaica*, viii.286.
33 See Doris Francis, *Will You Still Need Me, Will You Still Feed Me, When I'm 84?* (Bloomington: Indiana University Press 1984).
34 Mark Zborowski and Elizabeth Herzog, *Life Is with People: The Culture of the Shtetl* (New York: Schocken Books 1952), 290.
35 Ibid., 298.
36 Ibid., 203.
37 Geoffrey Alderman, *Modern British Jewry* (Oxford: Clarendon Press 1992), 14–15.

38 Melvyn Carlowe, 'Social Service', in Stephen Massil (ed.), *The Jewish Year Book 1996* (London: Vallentine Mitchell 1996), xlii–li.
39 Ibid., xlvi.
40 Ibid.
41 Peter Halfpenny and Margaret Reid, *The Financial Resources of the UK Jewish Voluntary Sector* (London: Institute for Jewish Policy Research 2000); Ernest Schlesinger, *Grant-making Trusts in the Jewish Sector* (London: Institute for Jewish Policy Research 2000).

3 The care system in the United Kingdom: formal provision for older people

The formal care provided to older people by public, voluntary and private sector organizations and agencies across the United Kingdom has, as Chapter 2 suggested, radically changed in recent years. These upheavals are set to continue and, in combination with predicted demographic changes, are providing major challenges for social care agencies and organizations. There are currently some 10.8 million people in the United Kingdom over the age of retirement: 3.9 million men over the age of 65, and 6.9 million women over the age of 60.[1] The Royal Commission established to examine the funding of long-term care services estimated that the cost (in 1995) for this industry was £11 billion: £7 billion from the state (NHS and social services) and £4 billion from older people themselves and their families. The Commission—using a model developed by the Personal Social Services Research Unit (PSSRU)—estimated that these costs would increase (at 1995–6 prices) to £14.7 billion in 2010, £19.9 billion in 2021, and £45.3 billion in 2051.[2] Almost half of all social services expenditure is on services to older people, and between 900,000 and 1.2 million people work in the social care industry in England (two-thirds of whom work in the independent sector, mainly in residential and nursing homes).[3] The formal care of older people is big business.

With the vast sums of money now required to provide the range of social care services for older people, many Jewish agencies and organizations have become increasingly integrated within the overall UK system. As such, what affects the United Kingdom as a whole also affects the Jewish community, and so providers need to understand the overall trends, systems and government policies that are likely to set the scene for how care is delivered and financed over the next decade. This chapter provides much of this information by detailing the current UK system of formal care provision for older people. The first part of the chapter examines demographic projections noting, in particular, the rapid increase in the number and proportion of older people over the next half century. The second part details the different types of care currently provided in the United Kingdom, setting out the national picture as a basis for comparison with provision that is specifically Jewish (see Chapter 4). The final part attempts to navigate some of the key New Labour social care legislation and initiatives that are shaping the future of social care services. This information is complex, but sets the scene for the changes the government is seeking to make. These changes include the imposition of national minimum standards for residential and nursing homes and alterations in how long-term care is funded. The government has also expressed interest in 'mainstreaming', i.e. encouraging the provision of services in general settings rather than by specific religious or ethnic minorities for their own communities. In combination, all these changes have important long-term implications for Jewish providers.

Demographic projections

Over the last century, the number of people in the United Kingdom has increased from just under 40 million to around 60 million. However, during this same period the number of people aged 60 or over has grown fourfold, from 2.87 million in 1901 to 12.2 million in 2001. Moreover, the number of people aged 80+ has increased elevenfold so that in 2001 there are almost as many people aged 80+ as there were aged 60+ in 1901 (see Table 3.1).

Table 3.1 **The changing number of older people in the UK over the last century**[4]

	Population (thousands)			
	60+	*70+*	*80+*	*All ages*
1901	2,876	1,066	218	38,237
1911	3,434	1,298	251	42,082
1931	5,314	1,962	376	46,038
1951	7,890	3,399	730	50,225
1961	8,973	3,954	1,017	52,709
1971	10,512	4,599	1,263	55,515
1981	11,020	5,438	1,485	55,089
1991	11,713	6,174	1,824	56,388
2001	12,201	6,765	2,481	59,954

With the increases in population over the last century and the high current annual expenditure on long-term care for older people—currently representing some 1.6 per cent of gross domestic product (GDP)—the government is unsurprisingly concerned with establishing likely future demographic trends. In terms of the overall population of the United Kingdom, this is likely to remain fairly static for the foreseeable future, increasing to 61.77 million in 2011, 63.64 million in 2021, and 64.1 million in 2051. Nevertheless, with rises in standards of living, advances in medical technology and the impact of the increase in birth rates after the Second World War and during the 1960s and early 1970s (the so-called 'baby-boomer' generations), the proportion and actual numbers of older people are expected to increase throughout the next sixty years (see Figure 3.1).[5] Figure 3.1 is drawn by

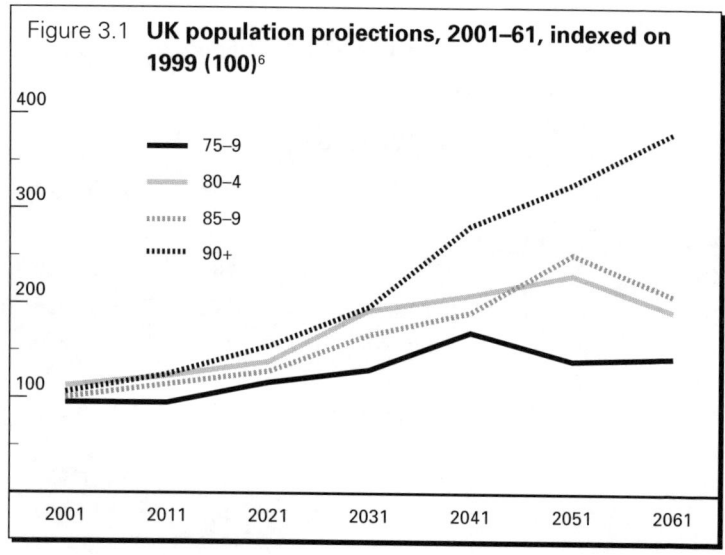

Figure 3.1 **UK population projections, 2001–61, indexed on 1999 (100)**[6]

indexing each of the age bands at a figure of 100 for the start year of 1999, so that the percentage change of each group can be compared. It shows how the numbers of individuals aged 75–9 will increase by a factor of 1.5 from 2001 to 2061; those aged 80–9 will more than double; but the most dramatic increases will be in those aged 90+, whose number will increase almost fourfold.

Figure 3.1 provides the best estimate to likely future demographic change. However, the relatively long period it covers makes it highly prone to error. The graph is calculated using known birth rates, and estimating future death rates based on assumptions about life expectancies for different age groups.

It is, however, almost impossible to calculate the likely effects on life expectancies of events such as future wars and diseases, as well as changes in medical technology and standards of living. Thus, a more realistic time period for the examination of demographic change is the next ten years. Figure 3.2 shows

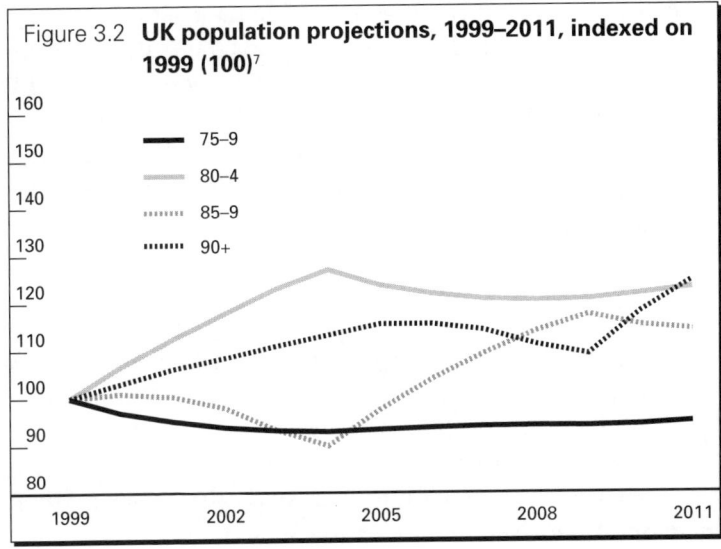

Figure 3.2 **UK population projections, 1999–2011, indexed on 1999 (100)**[7]

how numbers of people aged 75–9 will remain fairly static (or even decrease) over the next ten years; individuals aged 80–4 will increase by up to 30 per cent; those aged 85–9 will decline in number until 2004 before increasing again; and those aged 90+ will increase steadily until 2006, dipping slightly up to 2009 before increasing rapidly in 2010 and 2011.

An increase in the number of older people in the coming decades does not, of course, inevitably imply that there will be a corresponding rise in numbers requiring long-term care services.[8] One of the major debates in policy circles relates to changes in *healthy life expectancy*, defined as 'the years of life a person may expect to live free of some chronic health condition; or sometimes a related health state such as institutionalisation; or until the first occurrence of some crucial health event'.[9] For policy planning purposes, what matters most is the length of time that people are chronically ill (otherwise known as the morbidity rate), rather than their actual age.

Research from the PSSRU shows how there has been an average increase in life expectancies for men at 65 of 1.7 months for every year from 1980 to 1998; for women the figure is 1.2 months. For men, the average age by which they can no longer manage daily tasks on their own (such as bathing or showering, or getting to the toilet) has increased in line with these higher life expectancies (i.e. by 1.7 months for every year from 1980 to 1998). The age by which they can no longer manage to climb stairs on their own has increased by 1.5 months per year, to go outdoors unaided by 1.3 months, but the age at which they identify the onset of a long-standing limiting illness has risen by only 0.4 months. For women, their ability to manage daily tasks on their own has increased by 1.2 months per year (the same as their increase in life expectancy), to use stairs by 0.6 months and to go outdoors by 0.5 months, while the age at which they are likely to report a long-standing limiting illness has increased by 0.6 months. These figures suggest that older people are likely to have *more* years of mild and moderate levels of disability, i.e. to have a long-standing limiting illness or the inability to go outdoors unaided, than previous generations (who tended to become ill younger but also died earlier). In terms of severe disabilities (unable to manage daily tasks on their own), improvements in healthy life expectancies have kept pace with the dramatic increase in life expectancies witnessed over the past twenty years.

Overall, men can expect to live to 74, 16 years of which will be with limiting ill health; women can expect to live to 80, 20 years of which will be with limiting ill health.[10]

Related to the predicted rise in the number of older people will be a decrease in the proportion of those of working age to the rest of society. The basic state pension and the state earnings-related pension scheme (SERPS) are both funded through contributions of the current workforce, rather than from savings throughout the lifetimes of those who are now retired. Thus, a relative decline in the percentage of working-age people, in conjunction with an increase in the percentage of those above retirement age, has important implications for the funding of older people's services (see Figure 3.3). The number of people of pensionable age is estimated to increase from 29 per cent of those of working age in 2001, to 42 per cent in 2061.

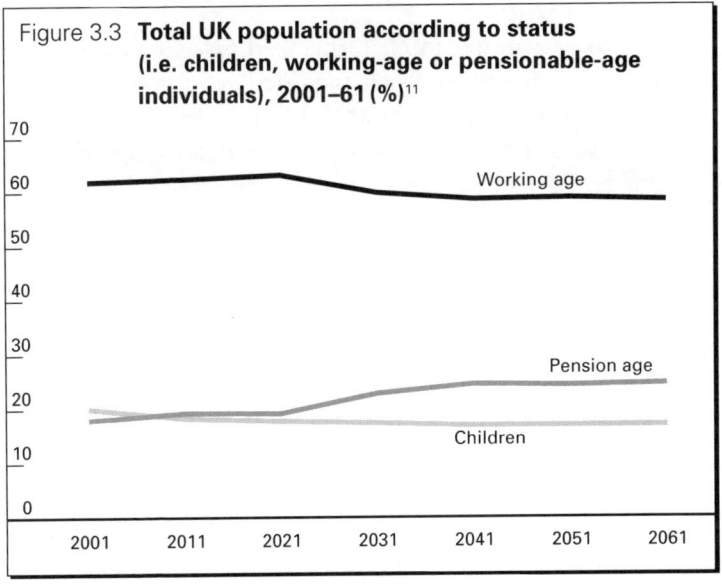

Figure 3.3 **Total UK population according to status (i.e. children, working-age or pensionable-age individuals), 2001–61 (%)**[11]

Different types of care

Most older people continue to live in their own homes and do not require any formal long-term care. As individuals become older, however, they are increasingly likely to make use of informal or unpaid care from spouses, relatives, friends and neighbours. About 5.7 million people in the United Kingdom provide some type of informal care, mostly for older people. Most of these people spend 4 hours or less per week providing unpaid care, although some 800,000 provide care for 50 hours a week or more. Sixty per cent of carers are women, with the largest type of care being that provided to parents or parents-in-law, mostly by people aged 45–64.[12] Nevertheless, nearly 1.6 million carers are over the age of 65 (and 400,000 are aged 75 and over), with 40 per cent of these individuals living in the same household as the cared-for person.[13]

For those requiring more formalized types of care, there are several different services provided in a range of care settings in the public, private and voluntary sectors. The 1999 Royal Commission on Long Term Care identified seven types of settings for formal care, although categories do overlap (see Table 3.2).

The most important services provided by the organized Jewish community are: *domiciliary care, day care centres, sheltered housing* and *institutional care*, especially residential and nursing care homes, which account for the lion's share of spending on long-term care for older people in the United Kingdom.

Domiciliary care

There are currently some 600,000 people in the United Kingdom over the age of 65 receiving domiciliary assistance

Table 3.2 **Care settings for older people**[14]

Care setting	Definition
Care at home (domiciliary care)	Personal care and practical help provided to older people in their own homes
Adult placement	Placing older people with selectively matched carers in carers' own homes
Day care	Including NHS day hospitals, local authority and independent sector day centres
Sheltered housing	Individual housing within a setting that offers varying degrees of monitoring, protection or support; either owned or rented; including very sheltered housing or housing with extra care, and retirement communities/care villages
Institutional care	In an institutional setting, either a residential or nursing home, provided by the public, private or voluntary sectors
NHS continuing care	In nursing homes, hospices and hospitals
NHS acute services	In NHS hospitals

from a local authority (see Table 3.3). Domiciliary care may include help with tasks such as washing and bathing, occupational therapy, community nursing and chiropody.

Of the approximately £11 billion spent on long-term care in 1995, £2.7 billion went on home care. As outlined in Chapter 2, government policy in recent years has been to keep people within their own homes for as long as possible. This is because most older people want to remain in their own homes (see Table 3.4), but also because supporting people in their own residence is generally considered to be more 'cost

Table 3.3 **Number of people in the UK receiving domiciliary care**[15]

Form of domiciliary care	Number of recipients
Home care	610,000
Community nursing	530,000
Private help	670,000
Meals	240,000

effective' than placing them in institutional care. The Royal Commission calculated typical costs per person for home care in 1999 at £6,188 per year (calculated at local authority rates of £8.50 an hour, 14 hours' help per week). This is approximately a third to a half of the annual cost of residential or nursing homes.[16]

As part of the drive to keep people out of institutional care there are grants available to help older people adapt their own homes. Under the Housing Grants, Construction and Regeneration Act 1996 older people can apply for a 'disabled facilities grant' for the installation of minor alterations, such as grab rails in bathrooms, as well as major changes, such as stair lifts or the construction of a downstairs bathroom. These adaptations can be enormously beneficial in improving the quality of life of many older people, although there is evidence of very long waiting lists for social service assessments and of reluctance by authorities to fund expensive changes (see also Chapter 9).[17]

Day care centres

Day care centres have evolved rather piecemeal, with 'little co-ordination between service providers, and great disparity in the level of provision between regions'.[18] Day care services

Table 3.4 **Preferences for formal and informal care**[19]

	Gross personal income per annum				
	<£6,000	£6,000–£11,999	£12,000–£19,999	£20,000+	All
Type of care	%	%	%	%	%
Relatives in your own home	19	16	13	8	15
Relatives in their home	4	3	1	–	3
Professionals in your own home	19	21	19	25	21
Nursing or residential home	12	11	11	12	12
Mix of family and professionals in your own home	42	45	55	53	47
Other	2	2	1	1	2

can be defined as offering 'communal care, with paid or voluntary caregivers present, in a setting outside the user's own home. Individuals come or are brought to use the services which are available for at least four hours during the day.'[20] About 260,000 people currently use day care services, which are provided in a variety of different settings, including generic day centres for older people, dementia-focused centres and day hospitals (including psychiatric day hospitals for older people). Local authorities provide approximately three-quarters of day centre places in England and Wales, with voluntary organizations providing the remainder.[21] Day care centres are vital tools in providing quality of life for individuals who may be suffering from loneliness or conditions such as

Alzheimer's disease or other forms of dementia. They are also important in providing respite for carers.

Sheltered housing

This is grouped accommodation that has some communal facilities such as a common room or laundry, a warden, and an alarm system to alert the warden in case of need. Schemes range from those accommodating fewer than 20 individuals to those with more than 100. The origins of sheltered housing date back to almshouses, although from the 1960s local authorities and housing associations increasingly provided them, attracted in part by large government subsidies. Since the 1970s, very sheltered housing schemes have also been developed. These are designed to meet the requirements of older people with care needs greater than those that can be accommodated in ordinary sheltered housing. These schemes tend to have more communal facilities, such as specialist baths for disabled people, twenty-four-hour warden cover and meals (provided once or twice a day). The boundary between very sheltered housing and residential care homes is often difficult to define. Five per cent of people aged 65 or over live in sheltered or very sheltered housing (see Table 3.5). There has been an increase in the average age of residents: in 1984 only one resident in ten was aged 85 or over, compared to almost one in four in 1993.[22]

Recent government advice has not been encouraging with regard to the construction of new sheltered housing, including very sheltered housing. The Housing Corporation—a non-departmental public body that funds and regulates Registered Social Landlords in England—has declared that new specialist housing schemes for older people will only be approved if evidence of housing and care needs can be clearly demonstrated. There seems to be

Table 3.5 **Provision of sheltered and very sheltered housing units for older people, England, 1997**[23]

	Local authorities	Housing associations	Other public sector	Private	Total
Sheltered housing	282,114	169,586	2,225	44,558	498,483
Very sheltered housing	7,134	9,873	1,034	–	18,041
Total	289,248	179,459	3,259	44,558	516,524

a greater desire to remodel existing schemes, rather than fund new schemes, as is clearly evidenced by the rapid fall in the construction of new dwellings for older people from 1989 to 1997 (see Table 3.6).

There is also evidence of the problem of obsolescent housing stock: properties that are difficult to let because, for

Table 3.6 **Number of new dwellings built for older people, England, 1989–97**[24]

	Private sector	Housing associations	Local authorities and new towns	Total
Sheltered				
1989	3,242	1,092	2,523	6,857
1993	808	1,442	202	2,452
1997	155	245	2	402
Other				
1989	554	339	1,004	1,897
1993	179	724	57	960
1997	45	113	11	169

example, they are studio apartments when what is needed is multi-bedroom housing. In 1994, 40 per cent of local authorities and 36 per cent of housing associations characterized between 1 and 9 per cent of their sheltered housing stock as 'difficult to let'. This problem is particularly acute in certain areas where 8 per cent of local authorities and 13 per cent of housing associations report that over half their stock is 'difficult to let'. There are also similar problems in letting very sheltered housing stock, with four-fifths of local authorities and housing associations describing between 1 and 9 per cent of their stock as 'difficult to let'.[25] According to the 1998 Audit Commission report, *Home Alone*:

> The principle of community care makes it harder to justify tying resources to property rather than people. Sheltered housing must accordingly re-invent itself as provision for older people who prefer the presence of a supportive community or it must re-think the levels of need it is able to support. If it does not it will face serious questions about its relevance in a system which can deliver high levels of support in ordinary housing.[26]

Housing associations are also faced with government standards and legislation requiring 'best value', with organizations having to prove the quality of services provided, for example through in-depth tenant satisfaction surveys.

Institutional care

There are currently over 480,000 older people residing in residential and nursing care homes, i.e. about 1 in 20 of all older people. The Royal Commission on Long Term Care calculates that one in five men, and one in three women, aged

65 or over, will require residential or nursing home care at some point in their lives. Residential homes provide meals and personal care such as help with washing, dressing, getting up and going to bed. Nursing homes provide personal care *and* specialist nursing care; they must employ qualified nurses and have at least one on duty at all times. Dual homes are combined residential and nursing facilities and these are also legally required to employ qualified nurses. Sixty per cent of long-term institutional care is provided in residential homes, 33 per cent in nursing homes and the remainder in hospitals (see Table 3.7). The costs of institutional care in 1995 were estimated to be £8.3 billion.[27]

Table 3.7 **Number of people in the UK receiving long-term institutional care**[28]

Institutional care	Number of recipients		Totals
Residential care	Publicly financed	205,000	288,750
	Privately financed	83,750	
Nursing home care	Publicly financed	115,000	157,500
	Privately financed	42,500	
Hospital		34,000	34,000
All institutional residents			480,250

The median average length of stay in a care home is estimated to be 19.6 months: 11.9 months for those originally admitted to nursing homes, and 26.8 months for residential care.[29] The factors at admission that significantly raise subsequent mortality rates are (in order of statistical significance): having a malignancy (cancer); having high levels of disability (low Barthel score); old age; being a man; being admitted from a nursing home; being admitted from a hospital; having a respiratory illness; and being cognitively impaired.[30]

In response to the recommendations of the Royal Commission, the care home sector is presently undergoing a major transformation. The overall thrust of the change is to increase the levels of care provided in people's own homes rather than in residential or nursing homes, to alter the way that private individuals pay for care, and to improve and standardize services in homes. These changes are part of an overall drive by the government to 'modernize' delivery of social care services.

New Labour social care legislation and initiatives

In 1998 the government published its White Paper, *Modernising Social Services*, which, in conjunction with *The NHS Plan* (2000) and the *National Service Framework for Older People* (2001), sets out to build social services that 'promote people's independence', 'improve protection of vulnerable people' and 'raise standards'.[31] In particular, the government hopes to effect change in six areas: assuring standards of care, extending access to services, ensuring fairer funding, developing services that promote independence, helping older people to stay healthy, and developing more effective links between health and social services. This section of the report introduces some of the key (primary and secondary) legislation and guidance initiatives that have been, and are being, introduced by the current New Labour government. In particular, it addresses three areas of particular relevance to the UK Jewish voluntary sector: *funding long-term care*, *regulations and standards* and *access to care and commissioning services*.[32]

Funding long-term care

The report by the Royal Commission on Long Term Care, *With Respect to Old Age*, was produced following fears of the spiralling costs to the state of residential and nursing care, and the concerns of older people (and their families) that they would need to sell their homes to pay for institutional care. The Commission made recommendations relating to the full spectrum of long-term care, from home services to residential and nursing care, but it was the latter that occupied most of its attention.

The costs of residential and nursing home care are divided between the state and older people themselves, with the relative amounts each has to pay determined by an assessment of the wealth of the person requiring care. This assessment is commonly known as the 'means test'. In 1997 just over 70 per cent of all residents in care homes were funded by the public sector in some way.[33] Following the recommendations of the Royal Commission, the government changed the way that private individuals pay for long-term care. Prior to April 2001 anyone with capital assets above £16,000 had to pay the full fees for care in a residential or nursing home.[34] In all other cases, in which people had capital assets of less than £16,000, individuals were expected to make a financial contribution towards fees. For those with capital between £10,000 and £16,000, an income of £1 per week for every £250 of capital was assumed, known as the 'tariff income'. Income from retirement pensions or income support was added to this tariff income, as a contribution towards fees. For those with assets below £10,000, only income from retirement pensions and income support was paid as a contribution. After the contribution towards fees, individuals were to be left with at least the amount of their 'personal expenses allowance'—often called 'pocket money'—which in 1999 was worth £14.45 per week. Following the government's changes, the system has been altered so that the nursing element of care is now (supposed to be) free and the value of a resident's home is disregarded during the first three months of care. The upper capital limit for paying full fees has now been raised to £18,500 and the lower capital limit to £11,500.[35]

The government's changes will improve the financial situation for many older people, although they fall short of the Commission's main recommendation that *all* personal care (including social care tasks, such as help with bathing) should be paid for from general taxation. It is worth noting, however, that in Scotland—which has devolved government—personal care is now free at the point of demand.

Another key change worth noting that emerges from the government's response to the Royal Commission is that the Residential Allowance in Income Support is to be transferred directly to local authorities (to be implemented from 2002, subject to parliamentary approval, for new cases only). The Residential Allowance is a payment to residents on income support in independent (private or voluntary) sector care homes, which means that a resident in their 80s outside of London could (in 1999) be entitled to £147.35 per week (almost twice that of a resident in a council home). Residents themselves do not benefit from this payment—it is counted as income to be contributed towards the payment of fees—with councils simply recouping the payment via the means test. However, it does encourage councils to use the independent sector for purely financial reasons, and can tip the balance between placing people in residential care and providing domiciliary care. By transferring this allowance straight to councils, this incentive for institutional care will be lost, and this may influence the numbers of individuals that local authorities choose to place into Jewish voluntary (and other independent) sector care homes.

Regulation and standards

A defining feature of successive governments over the past twenty years has been to introduce national regulations and standards for the local provision of services. In terms of education, for example, this includes the imposition of a national curriculum for all state schools, a national inspection system carried out by the Office for Standards in Education (OFSTED), and protection for pupils through a national database of individuals with criminal records involving children.[36] New Labour is continuing on this path in its programme for welfare services, including the introduction of the General Social Care Council to regulate the social care workforce, and national minimum standards to regulate care homes and other social services (including domiciliary care).[37]

Until recently, care homes located in the 150 local authorities and 100 health authorities, which were responsible for regulating and inspecting their services, were faced with major differences and inconsistencies in the standards they were expected to meet.[38] In March 2001 the government published the Care Standards Act 2000, which replaces the Registered Homes Act 1984 and is designed to implement national minimum standards (to apply mostly from 1 April 2002). These standards apply in seven key areas: choice of home, health and personal care, daily life and social activities, complaints and protection, environment, staffing, and management and administration. The National Care Standards Commission (NCSC), an independent non-governmental public body that has the power to determine the registration of services, will regulate these standards. Accordingly, care homes will be required to provide:

- an up-to-date statement of purpose for service users;
- each service user with a written contract/statement of terms and conditions;
- a service user plan of care for each resident;
- care and comfort to service users who are dying, handling their death with dignity and propriety, and observing their spiritual needs, rites and functions;
- communal space (apart from private accommodation, corridors and entrance halls) of at least 4.1 square metres for each service user (to apply from 1 April 2007 for homes existing prior to 1 April 2002);
- en-suite facilities (minimum of toilet and hand-basin) to all service users in all new buildings or extensions from 1 April 2002;
- a minimum of 12 square metres usable floor space in single rooms in all new buildings or extensions (excluding en-suite facilities);
- at least 10 square metres usable floor space in single rooms in current homes (from 1 April 2007);
- a minimum ratio of 50 per cent trained members of staff (NVQ level 2 or equivalent), to be achieved by 2005, excluding the registered manager and those care staff who are registered nurses;
- assurance by the registered person that there is a staff training and development programme that meets National Training Organisation (NTO) workforce training targets;
- a registered manager who has at least two years' experience in a senior management capacity and a qualification (by 2005) at NVQ level 4 in management and care or equivalent, or, where

nursing care is provided, who is a first level registered nurse and has a relevant management qualification (by 2005); and
- effective quality assurance and quality monitoring systems, based on seeking the views of service users, in order to measure success in meeting the aims, objectives and statement of purpose of the home; the results of service user surveys to be published and made available to current and prospective users, their representatives and other interested parties, including the NCSC.

These standards are designed to be minimum requirements for care homes, and indeed many already meet most of them. Nevertheless, the Care Standards Act 2000 is an attempt to improve standards and even out local variations in quality that have previously characterized the sector. The problem for many care homes is that, while standards are expected to rise, the financial support provided for those people who are unable to fund themselves is determined at the local level, with wide variations and inequalities (see below and Chapter 8). Investment in improving the standards of care homes—either through building new facilities or updating older ones—is necessarily a drain on communal resources. The fact that paying for these changes is a drain on organizations' reserve funds is compounded by the associated reduction in investment income, which forms an important element in charities funding the costs of running day-to-day services.[39]

Access to care and commissioning services
A third area of government legislation and policy guidance that is of crucial importance to the future of the UK Jewish voluntary sector relates to changes in the funding and

commissioning of services by local government. As Chapter 8 shows, arguably the most important strategic issue facing Jewish social care providers relates to the uneven funding of services by councils. Major changes in how councils commission services from independent (private and voluntary) sector organizations are under discussion, and these are likely to have important implications for Jewish providers. Moreover, there are important requirements for councils to ensure that the services they provide or commission are sensitive to issues of culture and faith.

Under the current system, central government provides 80 per cent of the funds for local councils to pay for social services, with monies provided in three main areas: 'older people', 'children' and 'other'. Central government provides funds to each council according to a Standard Spending Assessment (SSA)—with a cost adjustment to reflect those parts of the country where costs are higher—designed to determine the extent of local needs. With this pot of money councils are expected to provide or commission the social care services that they are statutorily required to deliver. However, the funds provided by central government for each of the three main areas are not 'ring-fenced', so that councils can, if they choose, spend some funds designed for older people on services for children or other groups. Indeed, the Royal Commission on Long Term Care calculated that local authorities spend an average of 16 per cent less than the SSA on services for older people, while spending more on younger disabled people and on children.[40] Moreover, there is currently no framework for councils to determine the eligibility criteria with regard to who should receive social care services; consequently, there are wide variations in the practices of different local authorities. To attempt to address these inconsistencies, the Department of Health has recently published a consultation draft, *Fair Access* to *Care Services* (*FACS*), which, when enacted, will provide guidance to councils for setting eligibility criteria by which individuals receive (or do not receive) local authority social care support.[41]

FACS is not designed to ensure that all councils operate the same eligibility criteria, but rather that people with similar circumstances living within the same council area should receive services that achieve 'broadly similar outcomes'. Councils are required to give priority to those individuals assessed as having greatest need, in terms of threats to their independence. Nevertheless, councils are entitled to take into account their available resources when setting eligibility criteria, although they should adopt a low threshold for entitlement. The eligibility criteria should be readily available and accessible to service users and published in local *Better Care, Higher Standards* charters.[42]

As part of these reforms, the government is seeking to change the nature of the relationship between councils and independent care providers. In terms of individuals funded by local authorities living in residential and nursing homes, most councils negotiate the actual amounts they are willing to pay per week with providers. Most councils in England fund clients in line with the amounts payable to individuals on 'preserved rights', i.e. those in institutional care before April 1993 who have centrally fixed rates of income support. As Chapter 8 shows, however, these amounts do not reflect the actual costs of providing institutional care. Clients entering residential and nursing homes are now much older and frailer than ever before, and therefore require greater, and thus more expensive, support. Moreover, many local authorities are overly concerned to reduce costs when they commission services, and thus pay even less than amounts consistent with those on preserved rights. Councils are required to operate under principles of 'best value', i.e. to commission services that are 'cost effective'. Unfortunately many councils—arguably due to overall funding shortages from central government (see below)—'bargain inappropriately', concentrating too much on minimizing costs rather than on the effectiveness of the services they are seeking to commission or provide.

In an attempt to minimize the threat to the care home industry from limitations in local authority funding, the government has launched a new agreement between the statutory and independent sectors, *Building Capacity and Partnership in Care*.[43] This aims to end the confrontational relationship between these two sectors and instead develop a partnership that places the needs of users and their carers at the centre of all decisions that are made. The upshot of these changes is that councils can be much more flexible in terms of the amounts that they pay to independent sector organizations, which should reflect the assessed needs of the clients they are funding. Of particular relevance to the Jewish community is that, under the Race Relations (Amendment) Act 2000 (which explicitly includes Jews)—and re-affirmed under the *National Service Framework for Older People* (2001) and *The NHS Plan* (2000)—provision of culturally appropriate care is 'not just good practice but a fundamental duty for councils and other statutory bodies'.[44] As such, councils are required to fund services that are culturally appropriate, and could—in theory at least—be legally challenged if they fail to do so.

In addition to all these changes, three other features of government direction are worth noting. The first is that, in line with thinking over the past forty years or more, the government is trying to enable people to retain their independence in their own homes for as long as possible. One of the latest initiatives is to encourage 'intermediate care', a range of care services that aim to prevent unnecessary hospital admission, provide effective rehabilitation services so that individuals can be discharged from hospitals early, and avoid premature or unnecessary admission to long-term residential care. Intermediate care services may include intensive support in people's homes by community nurses or therapy services, community equipment services, support to carers, and short-term 'step-up' care in residential or other settings. In addition, local councils are being encouraged to help people retain their independence through a 'promoting independence grant'. There is also the *Supporting People* initiative, designed to help vulnerable people live independently in the community by providing a wide range of housing-related support services.[45] The implications for the UK Jewish voluntary sector may be a decline in numbers in institutional care, but greater opportunities for short-term care and the further development of community services.

A second issue of particular relevance to the UK Jewish voluntary sector is government encouragement for the 'mainstreaming' of services. Issues relating to black and ethnic minority communities have been high on the government agenda, especially since the publication of the Stephen Lawrence inquiry report, with its damning indictment of institutional racism in the police force.[46] In 1998 the Department of Health and the Social Services Inspectorate (SSI) published *They Look After Their Own, Don't They?*, which examined services for black and other ethnic minority older people.[47] The Department of Health also has a series of initiatives called *Developing Services for Black Older People*, which developed from this publication, and attempts to improve a situation in which many ethnic minority people do not receive culturally appropriate and accessible social care services from local councils. However, the government's aim is to encourage the delivery of services to black and ethnic minorities within *mainstream* provision, rather than in 'segregated' environments.[48] This may have implications for service provision by the UK Jewish voluntary sector, although what these may be is, as yet, unclear. In addition, it is also worth noting that, in government discussions about ethnic minorities, the needs of the Jewish community are often completely ignored. The perception seems to be that the community is wealthy and has well-established voluntary organizations and, in the words of the SSI report, 'they look after their own'. The implications of such stereotyped thinking will be discussed in Chapter 9.

The third and final issue to be mentioned is the trend in overall government funding for social care services. Formal care for older people in the United Kingdom is a multi-billion pound industry, and radical improvements to service delivery may have considerable cost implications. In its 1998 White Paper on social services, the government promised an extra £3 billion over the following three years, including £1.3 billion for a Social Services Modernisation Fund. Nevertheless, the recent inquiry into care and support services by the King's Fund, *Future Imperfect?*, argued: 'It is apparent that the quality of care and support services falls far short of what users and carers should be able to expect. While a minority of services may be of a really poor standard, many are mediocre.'[49] As such, the report's first recommendation was for a massive boost in funding levels:

> We urge the Government to recognise the significant under-investment in care and support services, and to commit itself to making good the substantial shortfalls that have occurred year on year. We believe that the order of investment required is likely to be *at least the same* as that being injected into the NHS, i.e. a growth

of approximately half in cash terms, and one-third in real terms in just five years. Without such investment, care and support services will be struggling to stand still. They will be unable to address the major improvements needed in quality or to meet the additional requirements on new national standards.[50]

Conclusions

In recent years there have been enormous changes in the UK system of social care services for older people. These changes are set to continue and are driven by a combination of demographic, financial, political and social factors. Demographically, the number of older people in the United Kingdom is increasing, as indeed is their proportion relative to the (pre-65) working-age population. Estimating population trends is difficult, but the best estimates are that, while the increase in those aged 75–89 will peak in the middle of this century, the numbers of those aged 90+ will continue to rise for the foreseeable future. Moreover, those aged 90+ are the age group most likely to need formal care services.

Most older people will continue to live in their own homes, but for those who do require formal care, this can take place in a variety of settings, including people's own homes (domiciliary care), day centres, and residential and nursing homes. The annual costs for long-term care were estimated to be £11 billion in 1995, which could rise (at 1995–6 prices) to almost £20 billion in 2021 and to £45.3 billion in 2051. These spiralling costs have been a major impetus for reform, with the current New Labour government introducing an array of (often confusing) legislation, guidance and initiatives. The overall direction of government thinking is, however, to encourage people to remain independent in their own homes, to impose national standards on care services, and to balance the costs of maintaining (or developing) current provision with people's willingness to pay for it.

Notes

1. Note that the age of retirement for women will increase to 65 by 2020 (to be phased in over a 10-year period from 2010).
2. Royal Commission on Long Term Care, 8–22. Note that these figures do not include financial estimates for unpaid, voluntary work, which is a considerable element of the care given to older people. They are also based on assumptions about population growth, healthy life expectancies, care costs and levels of informal care.
3. Melanie Henwood, *Future Imperfect? Report of the King's Fund Care and Support Inquiry* (London: King's Fund 2001), 8–9.
4. Anthony Warnes, 'The demography of old age: panic versus reality', in Rosemary Bland (ed.), *Developing Services for Older People and Their Families* (London and Bristol, PA: Jessica Kingsley 1996), 26–42; 2001 figures from United Kingdom Government Actuary's Department (GAD).
5. See Maria Evandrou (ed.), *Baby Boomers: Ageing into the 21st Century* (London: Age Concern 1997).
6. Based on figures provided by GAD.
7. Based on figures provided by GAD.
8. For interesting critiques of ideas that older people are a 'demographic time bomb', see Phil Mullan, *The Imaginary Time Bomb: Why an Ageing Population Is Not a Social Problem* (London: I. B. Tauris 2000), and Warnes.
9. Andrew Bebbington and Adelina Comas-Herrera, *Healthy Life Expectancy: Trends to 1998, and the Implications for Long Term*

Care Costs, PSSRU Discussion Paper 1695 (London School of Economics), December 2000.
10 Bebbington and Comas-Herrera; see also Royal Commission on Long Term Care.
11 Based on figures provided by GAD.
12 Royal Commission on Long Term Care.
13 See Alison Milne, Eleni Hatzidimitriadou, Christina Chryssanthopoulou and Tom Owen, *Caring in Later Life: Reviewing the Role of Older Carers* (London: Help the Aged 2001).
14 Based on Royal Commission on Long Term Care, 83.
15 Ibid., 9.
16 Ibid., 26.
17 Francis Heywood, Christine Oldman and Robin Means, *Housing and Home in Later Life* (Buckingham: Open University Press 2002).
18 Julie Curran, 'The evolution of daycare services for people with dementia', in Rosemary Bland (ed.), *Developing Services for Older People and Their Families* (London and Bristol, PA: Jessica Kingsley 1996), 112–28 (112).
19 Table by C. Jarvis, R. Stuchbury and R. Hancock, reproduced in Henwood, 43. This table is based on responses given to the following question: 'Imagine that some time in the future you could no longer manage on your own and needed help with daily tasks such as getting up, going to bed, feeding, washing or dressing, or going to the toilet. How would you like to be looked after?'
20 S. Tester, quoted in ibid., 112.
21 S. Tester in 1989, quoted in ibid., 114.
22 Royal Commission on Long Term Care, Research Volume 2, 71.
23 Ibid., Research Volume 2, 69. Note that no distinction is made in figures for sheltered and very sheltered housing in the private sector.
24 Ibid., Research Volume 2, 70.
25 Ibid., Research Volume 2, 67–8.
26 Audit Commission, *Home Alone: The Role of Housing in Community Care* (London: Audit Commission Publications 1998), 28.

27 Royal Commission on Long Term Care.
28 Ibid., 9 and Research Volume 1, 14.
29 Because some residents will live for a long time, the mean average length of survival is much greater than the median, and is estimated at 29.7 months. Figures based on a longitudinal survey by the PSSRU of 2,629 care home admissions in 1995: Andrew Bebbington, Robin Darton, Royston Bartholomew and Ann Netten, *Survey of Admissions to Residential and Nursing Home Care: Final Report of the 42 Month Follow Up*, PSSRU Discussion Paper 1675 (London School of Economics), August 2000.
30 Ibid., viii.
31 Department of Health, *Modernising Social Services: Promoting Independence, Improving Protection, Raising Standards*, Cm 4169 (London: Stationery Office 1998); Department of Health, *National Service Framework*; Department of Health, *The NHS Plan*.
32 Note that most of the legislation and initiatives discussed in this section relate only to England—Wales, Scotland and Northern Ireland have separate legislation—where, in any case, the vast majority of Jews in the United Kingdom live.
33 Office of Fair Trading, *Older People as Consumers in Care Homes* (London: Office of Fair Trading 1998).
34 Assets generally include the value of older people's homes, although not if it is occupied by their spouse, partner or other specified relatives.
35 Department of Health, *The NHS Plan: The Government's Response to the Royal Commission on Long Term Care*, Cm 4818-II (London: Stationery Office 2000); see also Department of Health, *Moving into a Care Home: Things You Need to Know* (London: Department of Health Publications 1996).
36 See Oliver Valins, Barry Kosmin and Jacqueline Goldberg, *The Future of Jewish Schooling in the United Kingdom: A Strategic Assessment of a Faith-based Provision of Primary and Secondary School Education* (London: Institute for Jewish Policy Research 2001).

37 Department of Health, *Domiciliary Care: National Minimum Standards Regulations. Consultation Document* (London: Department of Health Publications 2001).
38 Department of Health, *Fit for the Future? National Required Standards for Residential and Nursing Homes for Older People* (London: Department of Health Publications 1999).
39 See Halfpenny and Reid.
40 Royal Commission on Long Term Care, 37.
41 Department of Health, *Fair Access to Care Services: Policy Guidance*, Consultation Draft (London: Department of Health Publications 2001).
42 Department of Health/Department of the Environment, Transport and the Regions.
43 Department of Health, *Building Capacity and Partnership in Care: An Agreement between the Statutory and the Independent Social Care, Health Care and Housing Sectors* (London: Department of Health Publications 2001).
44 Lydia Yee and Barry Mussenden, *From Lip Service to Real Service: The Report of the First Phase of a Project to Assist Councils with Social Services Responsibilities to Develop Services for Black Older People* (London: Department of Health Publications 2001), 21.
45 See Department of Health, *National Service Framework*, and Department of the Environment, Transport and the Regions.
46 William Macpherson, *The Stephen Lawrence Inquiry: Report of an Inquiry by Sir William Macpherson of Cluny* (London: Stationery Office 1999).
47 Social Services Inspectorate, *They Look After Their Own, Don't They?* (London: Department of Health Publications 1998).
48 See Yee and Mussenden.
49 Henwood, 138.
50 Ibid., 140.

4 The Jewish community's care system: formal provision for older people

Chapter 2 introduced the historical development of social care provision in the United Kingdom and discussed how Jews have traditionally cared for older members of their communities. Chapter 3 outlined the UK system of formal care provision for older people, including demographic projections, details of the different types of care provided, and key legislative and policy changes likely to affect directly the Jewish voluntary sector. This chapter builds on these discussions to map out the current system of *Jewish* formal care provision for older Jews living in the United Kingdom. This system reflects very strongly both the influences and financial realities of the UK social care sector as a whole, but also the particular circumstances of British Jewry, including the traditions, values and history of the community. Understanding this system, and having a baseline of current levels of provision, is key to any future planning and strategic decision-making.

The first part of the chapter discusses the demography of British Jewry, including projections of the numbers of Jewish older people and details of where Jews currently reside. In many ways Jews in the United Kingdom are demographic pioneers for the rest of society, in terms of higher proportions of older people, higher (on average) socio-economic status and lower birth rates. This demographic pattern is likely to be reflected across the whole of the population over the next two decades, so that issues being faced now by Jewish formal care providers are extremely relevant for planners outside the community. The second part of the chapter introduces the current range of services for older people provided by the UK Jewish voluntary sector, including meals-on-wheels services, day centres, sheltered housing and institutional care homes.

The current demography of British Jewry

The Board of Deputies of British Jews has collected data on Jewish births, deaths and marriages for over 150 years. According to the Community Research Unit (CRU) of the Board of Deputies, the UK Jewish population is currently estimated to be around 280,000.[1] However, estimating the population of British Jewry is a notoriously difficult task, given problems relating to definitions of 'who is a Jew' and the lack—until the most recent 2001 census—of a question on religion in the UK national census. Data for the 2001 census are not yet available and, in any case, there are questions as to what extent Jews chose to answer the religion question, which was voluntary. Many Jews see themselves as more an ethnic than a religious group and, as such, may not have given 'Jewish' as their answer to a question on religion (there is no category of 'Jewish' in the question on ethnicity). Some Jews may also have chosen not to give an answer either because they believe it is a state intrusion on their private lives or because they fear identifying themselves to government sources (despite very strict laws in place to protect the confidentiality of respondents).[2]

The CRU method for estimating population size is based on the number of deaths recorded in the Jewish community, on the assumption that anyone who lives as a Jew will want to be buried according to a Jewish rite. Nevertheless, it is important to note that British Jewry is not homogeneous, with several different branches including strictly Orthodox, central Orthodox, Masorti (Conservative) and Progressive (including Reform and Liberal) groupings. Approximately 70 per cent of the Jewish population are affiliated to a synagogue (either through personal or family membership). Of these Jews:

- 61 per cent belong to central Orthodox synagogues;
- 27 per cent belong to the Progressive sector (Reform and Liberal synagogues);
- 10 per cent to strictly Orthodox (Haredi) synagogues; and
- 2 per cent to Masorti (Conservative) synagogues.

Nevertheless, synagogue membership is not necessarily a precise indicator of religious lifestyle. Overall, one in every three British Jewish adults (31 per cent) think of themselves as 'traditional' Jews, 26 per cent 'secular', 18 per cent 'just Jewish', 15 per cent Progressive, and 9 per cent 'strictly Orthodox'.[3]

In addition to the CRU method for calculating the UK Jewish population, there are two other commonly used approaches that are worth mentioning. The first is based on *halakhah* (Jewish law), according to which a person is deemed Jewish only if they are born of a Jewish mother or else converted under the auspices of Orthodox authorities. Jews who convert under Progressive auspices are not considered 'legally' Jewish by Orthodox authorities, and thus would be excluded by this method. Moreover, this method includes people who may be considered 'legally' Jewish, but have no active connection or interest in Judaism and may thus choose never to make use of Jewish welfare services.

The second method is based on self-identification, with the assumption that anyone who considers themselves Jewish should be included in any total, regardless of questions of *halakhah*. However, while this is useful for obtaining a representative sample, it does not easily allow overall population rates to be calculated. All definitional approaches for counting Jews are problematic, with different methods useful for different purposes. As such, population figures and future demographic projections must be considered indicative, rather than definitive.

Figure 4.1 shows how the UK Jewish population increased steadily from 25,000–30,000 in 1850 to around 60,000 in 1880. From 1880 to 1915 the Jewish population increased by around 500 per cent, as large numbers of immigrants fled to Britain from state-sanctioned pogroms in Tsarist Russia.[4] Numbers of Jews continued to increase until the 1950s, reaching a peak of up to 430,000 (although recent research suggests that this is

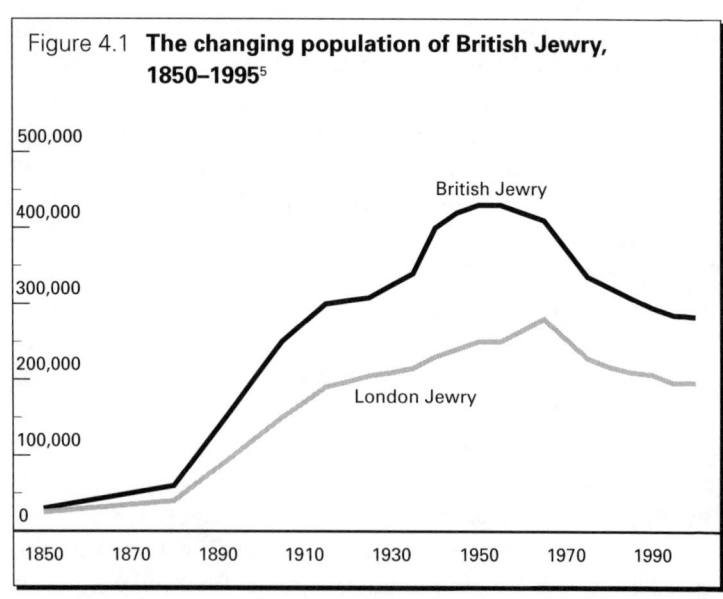

Figure 4.1 **The changing population of British Jewry, 1850–1995**[5]

probably an over-estimate). Since the 1950s numbers of Jews in the United Kingdom have shown a steady decline, with the population at the turn of the twenty-first century more than 25 per cent lower than that of fifty years ago. This decline is due to a combination of factors such as emigration, low fertility rates and assimilation resulting from the marriage of Jews to partners outside the Jewish community.

The latest data from the CRU show how numbers of births, deaths and marriages have all tended to fall over the last ten years. Births have fallen from over 3,300 in 1990, to around 2,500 in 1999. Burials and cremations under Jewish auspices have fallen from an average of 4,873 in 1975–9, to 3,791 in 2000. Marriages have also declined in recent years, so that in 2000 there were 907 synagogue marriages in the community, a slight decrease on the average of 947 for 1995–9. The decline in Jewish marriages parallels the situation in the United Kingdom as a whole, where national marriage rates have fallen by 3–4 per cent per annum since the early 1970s. The exception to this decline comes from the more Orthodox elements of the community so that the average age for first marriages in the more observant Union of Orthodox Synagogues is 6–7 years younger than in central Orthodox synagogues. The only vital statistic to show an increase in recent years is *gittim* (religious divorces), of which there were 269 in 2000. Finally, it is worth noting the regional variations in patterns of vital statistics. There are relatively more marriages and fewer deaths in London than in the regions, reflecting the higher proportions of older people in towns and cities outside the capital (see Table 4.1).[6]

In terms of the overall geographic distribution of the British Jewish population, it is estimated that there are over 80 towns and cities with identifiable Jewish populations, ranging from just a handful of Jews in places such as Newport, Torquay and

Table 4.1 **Synagogue marriages and deaths according to region, 2000**[7]

	London		Regions		Total
	Number	Percentage	Number	Percentage	
Marriages	674	74	233	26	907
Deaths	2,580	68	1,211	32	3,791

Dundee to 30,000 in Manchester and 196,000 in Greater London. Figure 4.2 shows this distribution, which highlights the wide range of areas populated by Jews, although around 50 of these towns have fewer than 300 Jews, and indeed several have populations of as few as 10 individuals.[8] Outside London, the greatest concentration of Jews is in Manchester, which has around 10 per cent of the UK Jewish population. Manchester's Jewish population has remained fairly constant over recent years, reflecting in particular a growth in numbers of strictly Orthodox Jews. The strictly Orthodox community has increased from a just a handful in the 1950s, to around 5,000 in 1999, mostly located in the Broughton Park and Prestwich districts of the city.[9] In contrast, almost all other regional communities have shown steady demographic decline. For example, up to 30,000 Jews lived in Glasgow immediately after the Second World War; this population has halved every generation since, and currently stands at less than 7,000.[10]

Greater London has the largest concentration of Jews in the United Kingdom, with most Jews living in the north-west part of the city. The borough of Barnet has the largest number of Jews in London at 50,000, i.e. 1 in 4 of all London Jews, or 1 in 6 of the total population of that borough. Hackney has the second largest number, with around 18,000 Jews, Redbridge 16,000, and Harrow 14,100. South of the River Thames there

THE JEWISH COMMUNITY'S CARE SYSTEM

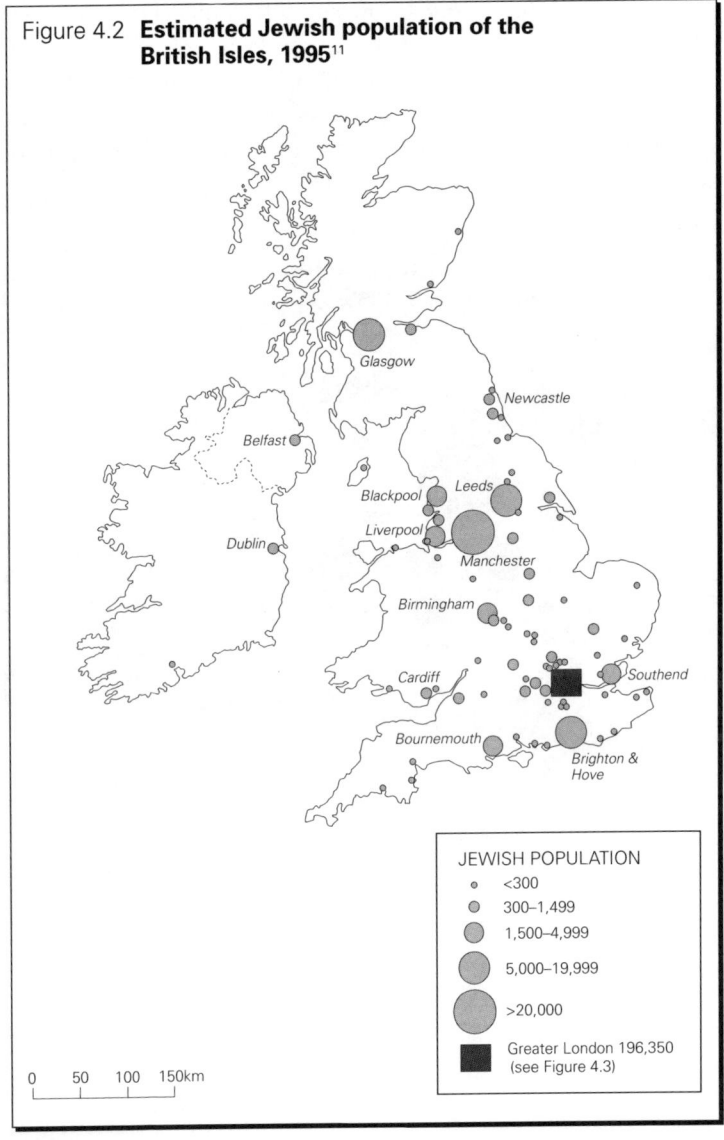

Figure 4.2 **Estimated Jewish population of the British Isles, 1995**[11]

are an estimated 16,400 Jews, who are fairly evenly distributed across the twelve boroughs (with a further 2,500 in North Kent and North Surrey). Outside the Greater London boundary, there is a sizeable population in South Hertfordshire (8,000 Jews), where two new Jewish primary schools have recently been established.[12]

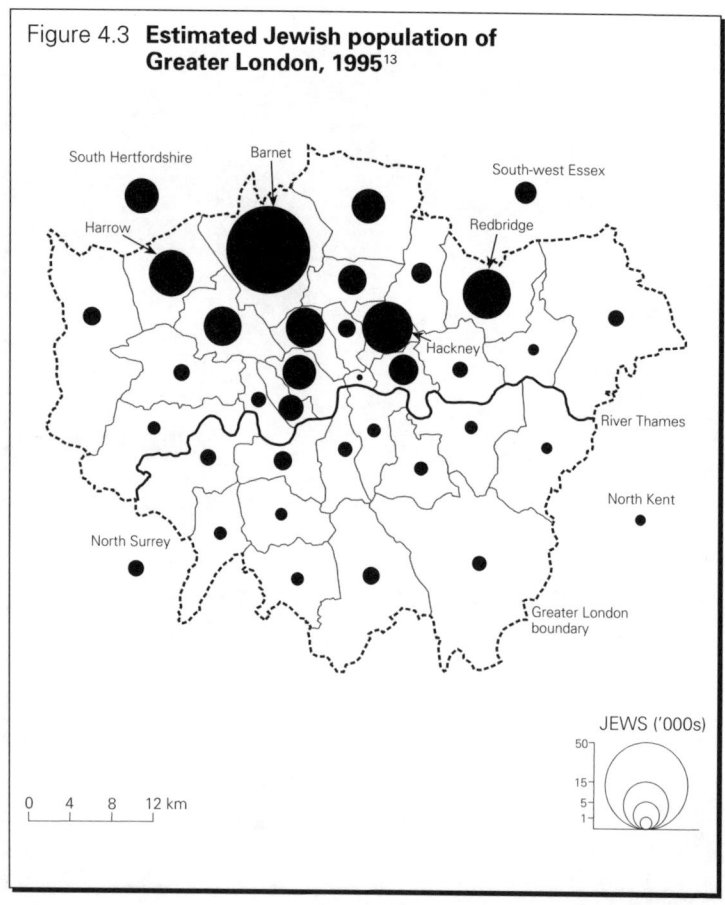

Figure 4.3 **Estimated Jewish population of Greater London, 1995**[13]

Demographic projections of older UK Jews

In terms of the numbers of older Jewish people in the United Kingdom, the CRU estimates that there are currently 63,000 Jews aged 65 or over, of whom some 38,000 are aged 75 or over. The number of Jews aged 75 or over is expected to remain relatively steady over the next ten years, although the numbers aged 90+ are expected to increase by 50 per cent to almost 8,000.

Table 4.2 **Projections of Jewish population 75+ based on government actuary death rates (death rates adjusted for social class)**[14]

Age	1999	2002	2005	2008	2011
75–9	11,900	12,600	11,500	11,500	12,200
80–4	11,200	10,200	10,900	10,000	10,100
85–9	9,000	8,500	7,800	8,400	7,800
90+	5,200	7,400	7,800	7,600	7,900
Total	37,300	38,700	38,000	37,500	38,000

If the figures from Table 4.2 are indexed at 100 for the start year of 1999—to show percentage changes over time—the rapid increase in the number of the 'oldest old' (Jews over 90) is evident, in contrast to the rest of the older population, which will stay relatively steady or decline over the next decade (see Figure 4.4). This contrasts notably with the overall UK population projections (see Figure 3.1), which suggest less dramatic increases in those aged 90 or over during the next ten years.

The demography of British Jewry differs markedly from the United Kingdom population as a whole. These differences are

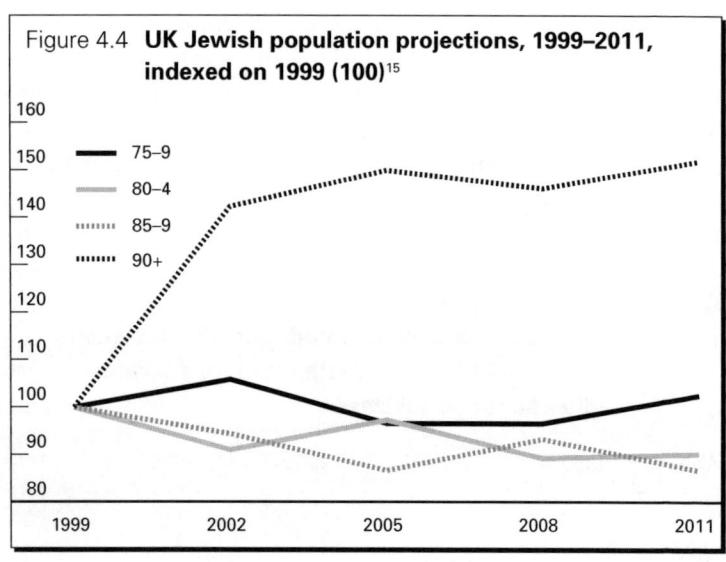

Figure 4.4 **UK Jewish population projections, 1999–2011, indexed on 1999 (100)**[15]

due mainly to the fact that British Jews tend to be of above average socio-economic status, with 54 per cent of working Jewish men and 50 per cent of working Jewish women in professional and managerial occupations, compared with 10 per cent of men and 8 per cent of women in the general population.[16] Socio-economic status is closely linked to demography: those in the higher brackets are likely to live longer and have fewer births. Some 23 per cent of British Jews are 65 or over, compared with 16 per cent in the United Kingdom as a whole. Approximately 14 per cent of British Jews are aged 75 or over, as opposed to 7 per cent of the general population.[17] Forty-one per cent of Jews are aged 35 or under, compared with 48 per cent in England and Wales. In 1989–93 the average (median) age of death was 79 for Jewish men and 82 for Jewish women, compared with 73.6 and 79.6 respectively for England and Wales.[18]

The future demography of British Jewry is likely to be affected by three further particular attributes of the community. The first is the effect of a history of emigration, particularly to Israel and the United States, which means that a proportion of Jews born in the United Kingdom will not be living in the country when they are older. The second factor is the impact of inter-marriage, with 44 per cent of men under the age of 40 marrying non-Jewish women.[19] There are questions as to whether these individuals and their spouses will want Jewish social services when they are older, and the extent to which Jewish agencies will accommodate them if they do (see Chapter 9). The third factor is the impact of the rapid increase in recent years of the percentage and overall numbers of strictly Orthodox Jews. In 1995 it was estimated that strictly Orthodox Jews accounted for around 10 per cent of the Jewish population; however, with much higher fertility rates—having 7, 8 or 9 children is common—their share is expected to increase. Indeed, the number of children in strictly Orthodox schools and nurseries has almost doubled over the last ten years, accounting for 43 per cent of the total number of Jews attending Jewish day schools.[20]

Current provision of services to older people

The Jewish voluntary sector is similar to the overall system of welfare for older people in the United Kingdom in that it provides a range of services, from meals-on-wheels to sheltered housing, day care centres to institutional care. Thousands of paid and unpaid (volunteer) staff help deliver these services every week, which are provided by dozens of different organizations and agencies. Indeed, across the UK Jewish voluntary sector there are almost 2,000 financially independent organizations, operating in fields as diverse as education, religion, culture and social care. Financially, social care is the single largest component of this sector, accounting for 27 per cent (£135 million) of the total income.[21] This part of the chapter details some of the key elements of this system (domiciliary services and day centres, sheltered housing and institutional care). First, however, it is important to recognize the semi-formal levels of care that are also provided by the Jewish community.

The Jewish community provides a range of such semi-formal activities every week, making differing levels of care available to older Jews or others requiring community assistance. For example, synagogues across the religious spectrum provide luncheon or friendship clubs for older people. The Association of Jewish Friendship Clubs co-ordinates the activities of around 50–60 such clubs, which provide speakers, entertainment, activities and welfare information for several thousand people aged 60 or over. Other semi-formal organizations—likewise often linked to individual synagogues and rabbis—include those for visiting the sick or arranging kosher meals in hospitals, bereavement counsellors and burial societies.[22] The most extensive networks of semi-formal charitable services for British Jews are, however, to be found in the strictly Orthodox communities.

The United Kingdom contains four main strictly Orthodox communities: Gateshead; Broughton Park in Manchester; Golders Green/Hendon in North-west London; and Stamford Hill in North-east London. These communities all have their own systems of self-help so that, in Broughton Park, for example, there is a *hesed* (literally 'kindness') list that offers a range of over 120 items available for members to borrow, or services to use, free of charge. The *hesed* list works through people volunteering items for loan, with the details collated, printed and distributed to community members. The list is updated every twelve months or so, and anyone wishing to make use of the facilities simply telephones the number of the person who runs the particular service, and makes the arrangements, such as when and where to collect/return the items borrowed. Items that can be borrowed range from crockery and cutlery, to medical equipment such as wheelchairs and breathing monitors. In addition, the community also runs its own ambulance service called *hatzolla*. This is a network of trained first-aid workers and on-call doctors who can be contacted by telephone at any time of the day or night, providing rapid medical care for those in need. This semi-formal system, which is delivered at the local level, is one important way in which the community supports individual members.[23]

Domiciliary services and day centres

While institutional care accounts for the lion's share of spending on formal older people's services, far more people actually make use of domiciliary services and/or attend day centres run by communal Jewish organizations. Across the United Kingdom there are twenty-one formal Jewish day centres for older people, which cater for approximately 3,000 Jews each week. These are open for different periods of time, from only one day a week to six. Some are independent, while others are run by larger community organizations such as Jewish Care, the League of Jewish Women and the Association of Jewish Refugees. Some of the larger ones provide transportation for users, and nearly all provide a kosher lunch as well as tea, coffee and biscuits throughout the day. The day centres typically offer a range of activities such as quizzes, bridge clubs, exercise classes, discussion groups and entertainment sessions. Some larger day centres—such as some of those run by Jewish Care—may even have such facilities as a gift shop (selling items such as greeting cards and toiletries), a reminiscence room, a dress shop, a hairdressers, a chiropody service, a television room, a library, and arts and crafts workshops. Most day centre users reside in their own homes, but some also come from residential and nursing homes; indeed, a couple of day centres are based in care homes.

Alongside ordinary day centres, there are a also a small number of facilities especially designed to cater for older people suffering from confusion, including dementia (such as Alzheimer's disease). These centres are similar to ordinary day centres, and typically provide transportation, personal care (such as bathing and chiropody), kosher meals, and visits and activities. Nevertheless, they are able to cater for these older people in a more therapeutic manner and to support their carers.

In addition to day centres, the Jewish community offers a range of services that can be provided in people's own homes. These include kosher meals-on-wheels services, which is one of the most traditional forms of UK Jewish charitable activity. These meals are cooked and distributed by a range of different agencies, including day centres, local charities and organizations such as Jewish Care and the League of Jewish Women. Some of these services are paid for by local authorities, while others are voluntarily donated by Jewish charities. Somewhere in the region of 1,700–3,000 meals are distributed each week by Jewish organizations, although the precise figure is difficult to determine given that many organizations are uncertain as to how many they deliver and whether they are in partnership with other agencies (which would result in double counting). Cities such as Manchester and London have multiple providers, with, it seems, relatively little co-ordination between them: there is little or no attempt to reduce costs through bulk purchasing or to co-operate with regard to what should be paid by the community and what by local councils. In addition, some local authorities provide kosher services directly (independently of Jewish charities) and there is also a Hospital Kosher Meals Service that provides 3,000–4,000 meals per week to Jewish patients of all ages. The difficulty in obtaining information from meals-on-wheels providers suggests an urgent need for them to work together and to share ideas, thus avoiding any wasteful duplication of time and services (see Chapter 9).

Cities with a sizeable Jewish population also have dedicated Jewish social service agencies that are able to provide or organize domiciliary services. In Greater London and the South-east, Jewish Care runs a range of services, such as the KC Sasha Centre, which records the *Jewish Chronicle* newspaper, Jewish-type books, newsletters and items of interest on to audio tapes for the use of the blind and partially sighted. There are also dedicated social workers who assess and can arrange for the social care needs of older people (and other members of the community). Social workers may help people with a range of activities from moving home (for example, to sheltered accommodation or a care home) to organizing kosher meals-on-wheels. Jewish Care also runs the Kennedy Leigh Home Care service, which consists of a team of trained care assistants who help people remain independent in their own homes. Services provided include personal care (such as bathing and dressing), practical assistance in the home, shopping, preparing meals and escorting clients to hospital appointments. Jewish Care also runs an Admiral Nurse Service (admiral nurses are able to assist and support carers looking after someone with memory problems, confusion, Alzheimer's disease and other forms of dementia by providing information and advice). Indeed, many Jewish social service agencies are trying to cater more for the needs of carers, such as Project Smile run by the Manchester Jewish Federation.

Sheltered housing

Twenty-four Jewish organizations are members of the National Network for Jewish Social Housing, the majority of which provide dedicated housing for older people. These organizations have a total stock of around 4,000 flats and houses, just under three-quarters of which are based in the Greater London area. Jews currently occupy around 2,700 of these units. The largest single provider is the Industrial Dwelling Society with over 1,200 units, although Jews occupy only one-fifth of these. Bnai Brith JBG is the largest provider of specifically Jewish social housing, with over 95 per cent of its total stock of more than 650 units occupied by Jews. Other major providers include Jewish Blind and Disabled (JBD), the strictly Orthodox Agudas Israel Housing Association (AIHA) and, outside London, Leeds Jewish Housing Association, Liverpool Jewish Housing Association and Glasgow Jewish Housing Association. Around half of the stock is designated for older people, while the rest is mixed social housing (see Tables 4.3 and 4.4).

Table 4.3 **Total housing units of UK Jewish housing associations, 2000**

	Number of organizations	Total housing units	Units occupied by Jews
London and South-east	16	2,870	1,740
Regions	8	1,100	925
Total	24	3,970	2,665

Table 4.4 **Units for older people held by UK Jewish housing associations, 2000**

	Older people housing units	Older people units occupied by Jews
London and South-east	1,310	1,160
Regions	700	565
Total	2,010	1,725

Institutional care

In terms of residential and nursing homes, there are 21 separate organizations, providing care for older people in 36 homes (see Table 4.5). There are more organizations in the regions providing care than in London and the South-east, although the capital has, by far, the largest number of facilities. This reflects the dominance of Jewish Care in the South-east, which, as a single organization, provides almost two-thirds of Jewish voluntary sector bed spaces in the capital. In Manchester there are four separate organizations providing care facilities, while Birmingham, Bournemouth, Cardiff, Glasgow (with two homes), Leeds, Liverpool, Newcastle, Nottingham and Southport each have one.

Table 4.5 **Number of organizations and homes providing residential and nursing care in the UK Jewish voluntary sector, 2001**

	Number of organizations	Number of homes
London and South-east	8	22
Regions	13	14
Total	21	36

In terms of the overall distribution of registered places, there are currently almost 2,500 bed spaces available in Jewish residential and nursing voluntary sector care homes (see Table 4.6). Thus, around 1 in 25 Jews aged 65 or over are in long-term Jewish voluntary sector care homes, with many others in private facilities (see later). Approximately two-thirds of the registered bed places in the UK Jewish voluntary sector are classed as residential, with regional communities having more bed spaces per person than in London and the South-east: around 75 per cent of all UK Jews live in London and the South-east, but only 62 per cent of registered places are located there. Much of this imbalance is due to numbers of nursing home places, with the regions having a much higher proportion of nursing beds relative to residential beds than in London and the South-east. The pattern of London and the South-east (one nursing bed for every two residential beds) is in line with the United Kingdom as a whole (see Table 3.7). The reasons why regional areas have many more nursing places is not clear, but may simply reflect a historical tradition in these areas for offering nursing care.

Table 4.6 **Residential and nursing homes in the UK Jewish voluntary sector, 2000**

	Residential places	Nursing places	Total registered places
London and South-east	1,050	485	1,535
Regions	540	420	960
Total	1,590	905	2,495

Figure 4.5 shows the distribution of care homes in Britain according to the size of individual institutions and whether

THE JEWISH COMMUNITY'S CARE SYSTEM

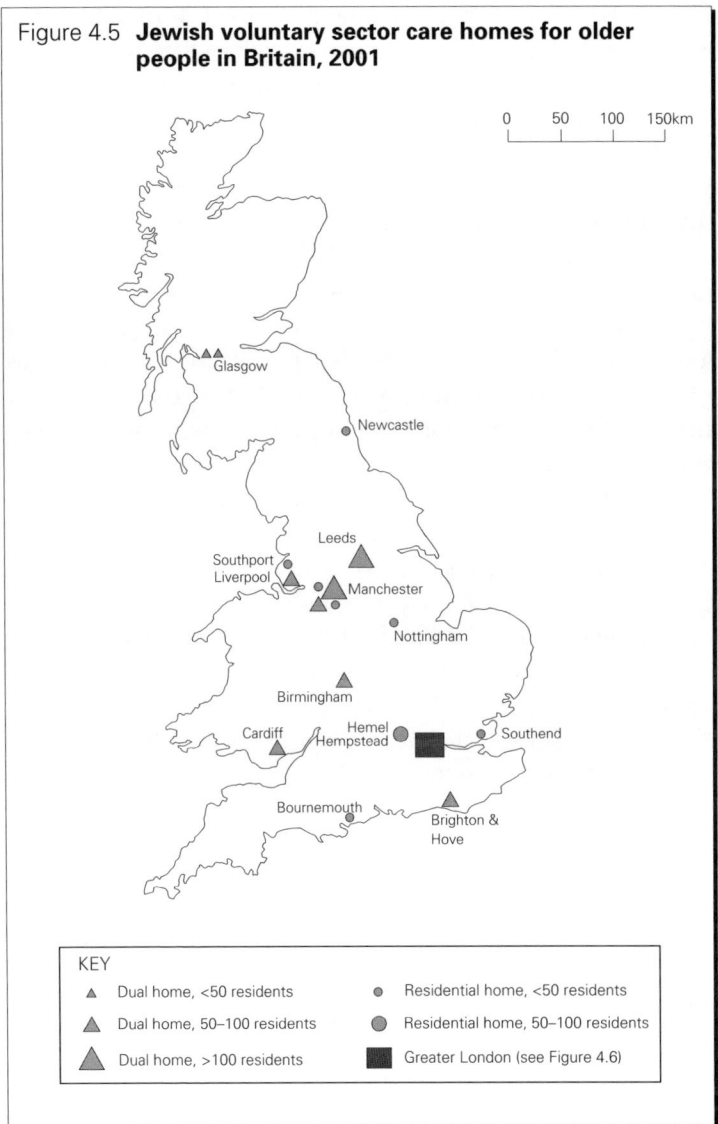

Figure 4.5 **Jewish voluntary sector care homes for older people in Britain, 2001**

they provide residential, nursing or dual forms of care. When compared with Figure 4.2 it is clear that most towns with a sizeable Jewish population have at least one care home. The two largest homes in the regions are Heathlands in Manchester, which has places for more than 250 residents, and Donisthorpe Hall in Leeds with over 180. This compares to the average number of places in England of 12 in independent residential homes, 29 in all local authority homes, 37 in nursing homes, and 40 in dual registered homes.[24] Cardiff, Newcastle, Nottingham and Southport, which all have Jewish populations of less than 1,500, still manage to support a care home. The survival of these institutions in what were once cities with much larger Jewish populations reflects the fact that in declining regional towns and cities older Jews are more likely to remain than younger Jews. The population is thus weighted in terms of older people and hence the market for long-term care remains (at least in the short term). These homes are also likely to draw in residents from surrounding areas, although some are also now taking in non-Jewish residents for the first time (see Chapter 8).

Figure 4.6 shows the distribution of voluntary sector care homes in Greater London. This map demonstrates the remarkable concentration of homes in the north-west sector of the city, with 14 of the 19 London homes within 8 kilometres of each other, mostly in the southern part of Barnet. There are two further homes in Hackney (including the AIHA Beis Pinchos home that caters specifically for the strictly Orthodox community), one in Redbridge and one in Brent. South of the river, the only home is the very large Nightingale House, which is apparently the largest home for older people in Europe with over 300 residents. It is noticeable that the London borough of Harrow (14,100 Jews)

THE JEWISH COMMUNITY'S CARE SYSTEM

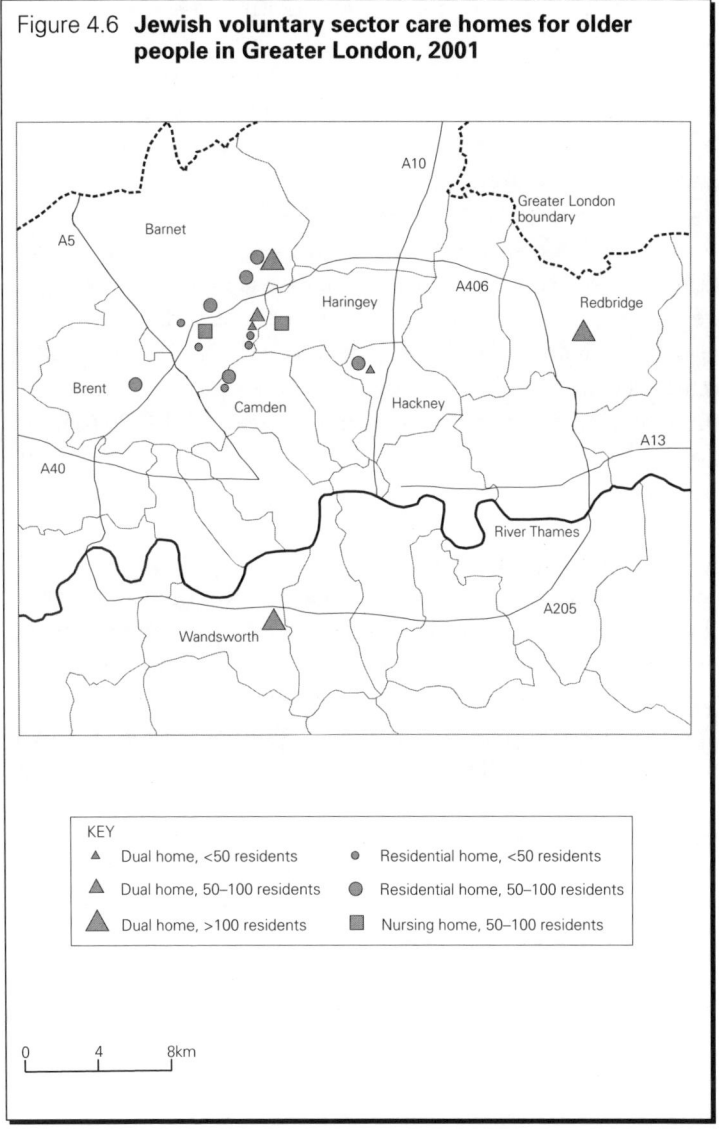

Figure 4.6 **Jewish voluntary sector care homes for older people in Greater London, 2001**

does not have a care home, and neither does South Hertfordshire (8,000 Jews).

Within Greater London, a report by Michael Jimack showed that in 1992 there were 1,572 long-term residential and nursing beds in the Jewish voluntary sector. This is very similar to the current situation, although Jimack did expect the number of beds to increase to 1,739 by 1994.[25]

Also of interest are the average ages of clients in Jewish voluntary sector care homes, with the mean average being 88 years old, and indeed almost 90 in the London area. This compares with England as a whole, where 75 per cent of residents are aged 80 or over, but represents a large rise compared to a generation ago. In the 1960s and 1970s service providers in Jewish voluntary sector homes noted the average age of residents as being closer to 70; indeed, some residents used to drive their own cars. This change reflects new government funding regulations for long-term care and different attitudes towards care among the public, as well as the fact that the functional abilities of older people are being maintained longer through improved medical and domiciliary services. To gain local authority funding for long-term care, residents have to be shown to have ever-greater levels of need; thus clients tend to be older, frailer and have higher levels of disability or long-standing illness. The Department of Health estimates that just over 50 per cent of older people in care homes have cognitive functioning problems (for example, Alzheimer's disease or other forms of dementia), compared with only one per cent of the older population generally.[26] Unsurprisingly, care homes have many more female residents than male, with an overall average of 28 per cent males and 72 per cent females in Jewish voluntary facilities (see Table 4.7). This is similar to England as a whole, where 76 per cent of those aged 65 or over in care homes are female.

Table 4.7 **Average age and percentage of female clients in Jewish voluntary sector care homes, 2000**

	Age of clients (male and female)	Percentage of female clients
London and South-east (mean) average	90	71
Regions (mean) average	85	80
Range	78–95	55–90
Overall (mean) average	88	72

In addition to care homes in the Jewish voluntary sector—those run by not-for-profit Jewish organizations—there are also many private homes in which Jews live. As Chapter 2 showed, there has been a rapid increase over the last twenty years in the number of independent (private and voluntary) care homes: in 1999, just over 90 per cent of residential care homes in the United Kingdom as a whole (and 83 per cent of places) were in the independent sector.[27] Michael Jimack's report on the Jewish system of care estimated that, in those London boroughs where large numbers of Jews live, there were 34 homes that catered for almost 1,100 Jewish residents. Jimack noted that these homes varied considerably in how they catered for Jews, with the majority limiting their activities to providing either kosher meals (cooked by external Jewish catering firms) or a vegetarian diet.[28]

An analysis in 2001 of the 38 private care homes in the borough of Barnet showed that these had 1,048 registered places (625 residential and 423 nursing). Jews occupied just over one-quarter of these places, approximately 175 in residential facilities and 115 in nursing homes. Only three members of staff in these homes were Jewish. Although most of the homes stated that they could provide kosher food, many did not provide Jewish social and cultural activities on the premises but were prepared to transport residents to local Jewish day centres or synagogues if this was requested. Nevertheless, around two-thirds of the Jews living in private facilities are accounted for by five care homes that have a majority of Jewish clients. These homes provide much more in the way of Jewish activities (and kosher food) than do the others. In addition, there are also some 591 registered places in non-Jewish voluntary sector homes in Barnet, of which around 20 are currently occupied by Jews.

Overall, Barnet has 741 registered places in Jewish voluntary sector homes (530 residential and 211 nursing), with a further 310 Jews living in private facilities or non-Jewish voluntary sector homes. Thus, there is an approximate ratio of seven Jews in Jewish voluntary sector homes for every three in private or non-Jewish facilities. If this pattern is reflected across the United Kingdom, then around 1 in 19 older Jews are currently living in residential or nursing homes (whether voluntary or private, Jewish or non-Jewish). This figure is similar to the overall ratio of 1 in 20 for England and Wales as a whole (see Chapter 3).

Conclusions

Planning for the future directions of the UK Jewish voluntary sector requires a complex assessment of a range of factors, including the changing aspirations and expectations of the population, government legislation and available resources. Nevertheless, two of the key elements are the probable demographic changes and the system of care currently being provided. In terms of demographics, the Board of Deputies of British Jews calculates that over the next ten years the number of Jews aged 75–89 will remain fairly steady, or even decrease slightly, but that there will be a large increase in the number of those aged 90+ (the age group most likely to need formal care services). At first sight these demographic changes suggest a need for an increase in sheltered housing and institutional provision by the Jewish community. However, when other factors of the equation are considered—especially the impact of current and future government legislation—such growth is likely to be more than mitigated. There is an extensive system of care services provided by Jewish community organizations across the United Kingdom, from meals-on-wheels to day centres, domiciliary social services to institutional care. The future of these services is dependent on the financial and volunteer support from an ever-reducing number and proportion of economically active Jewish citizens.

Notes

1. Schmool and Cohen.
2. See Barry Kosmin, *Ethnic and Religious Questions in the 2001 UK Census of Population: Policy Recommendations* (London: Institute for Jewish Policy Research 1999).
3. See Commission on Representation of the Interests of the British Jewish Community, *A Community of Communities: Report of the Commission on Representation of the Interests of the British Jewish Community* (London: Institute for Jewish Policy Research 2000).
4. See Alderman; Lloyd Gartner, *The Jewish Immigrant in England 1870–1914* (London: Simon Publications 1973); and Henry Pollins, *Economic History of the Jews in England* (London: Associated University Presses 1982).
5. Data taken from Stanley Waterman and Barry Kosmin, *British*

Jewry in the Eighties: A Statistical and Geographical Study (London: Board of Deputies of British Jews 1986), and Schmool and Cohen.

6. Board of Deputies of British Jews, *Report on Community Statistics for 2000* (London: Board of Deputies of British Jews 2000); Board of Deputies of British Jews, *Report on Community Statistics for 1999* (London: Board of Deputies of British Jews 1999).
7. Board of Deputies of British Jews (2000).
8. Data from Stephen Massil (ed.), *The Jewish Year Book 2001* (London: Vallentine Mitchell 2001).
9. Oliver Valins, 'Identity, Space and Boundaries: Ultra-Orthodox Judaism in Contemporary Britain', Ph.D. thesis, University of Glasgow, 1999.
10. See Kenneth Collins, *Second City Jewry* (Glasgow: Scottish Jewish Archives 1990); Elaine Samuel and Charlotte Pearson, 'The Jewish community of Greater Glasgow: population and residential patterns', Department of Social Policy, University of Edinburgh, 1999.
11. Map drawn from data in Massil (ed.). Note that the Board of Deputies is currently updating its UK Jewish demographic projections and population statistics, but these were unavailable at the time of writing.
12. Schmool and Cohen.
13. Map drawn from data in Schmool and Cohen.
14. Data from the Board of Deputies of British Jews.
15. Data from the Board of Deputies of British Jews.
16. Stephen Miller, Marlena Schmool and Antony Lerman, *Social and Political Attitudes of British Jews: Some Key Findings of the JPR Survey* (London: Institute for Jewish Policy Research 1996).
17. The percentage of people aged 75 or over in the United Kingdom as a whole has increased from 4 per cent in 1971 to 7 per cent in 1998: see Office for National Statistics, *Living in Britain: Results from the 1998 General Household Survey* (London: Stationery Office 2000).

18 Schmool and Cohen.
19 Miller, Schmool and Lerman.
20 Valins, Kosmin and Goldberg; see also Oliver Valins, 'Institutionalised religion: sacred texts and Jewish spatial practice', *Geoforum*, vol. 31, 2000, 575–86.
21 Halfpenny and Reid.
22 See, for example, United Synagogue, *Care Matters: A Directory of Information for Care Providers in the United Synagogue* (London: United Synagogue 2001).
23 Valins, 'Identity, Space and Boundaries'.
24 Department of Health, *Community Care Statistics 1999: Residential Personal Social Services for Adults, England*, Statistical Bulletin 2000/2 (London: Department of Health Publications 2000).
25 Michael Jimack, *Residential Care and Nursing Provision for the Elderly in the Greater London Jewish Community* (London: Jewish Care 1992).
26 UK figures from Department of Health, 'Health survey for England: The health of older people—First release tables', press release, 29 June 2001.
27 Department of Health, *Community Care Statistics 1999*.
28 Jimack.

5 The potential social care marketplace: older Jews living in Leeds

Chapters 2–4 explored some of the key data and informational inputs needed for effective strategic planning for the future of Jewish social care services. However, strategic planning requires much more than demographic data and details of current service provision; it also involves an understanding of the current and future populations likely to need Jewish social care services. This chapter presents key aspects concerning these populations, using quantitative data provided by 1,500 adults—one-quarter of whom were aged 75 or over—in response to a questionnaire sent out to Jews living in the city of Leeds, the first stage of JPR's National Survey of British Jewry (see Preface). The resulting Leeds Jewish Community Study provides a fascinating glimpse into the characteristics of Jews living in a northern regional city, and is an important case-study of a minority population. The survey was designed to access the 'voices' of people who are likely to be the current and future recipients of Jewish voluntary sector services, and to ascertain needs and aspirations regarding key communal social services, especially education, housing and care for older people and those who are infirm. This chapter presents the findings from an initial analysis of the section of the population aged 75 or over.[1] This is the section of the population most likely to be using domiciliary services, as well as the potential future market for institutional care. Issues relating to those already within institutional care settings (who were not covered by the survey) are specifically discussed in the following three chapters. The chapter begins with a brief introduction to the historical development of the Leeds Jewish community, before moving on to discuss the current population as described in the questionnaire responses. In particular, this chapter considers: general and income characteristics, Jewish attitudes and practices, the health of older Leeds Jews, mobility, and current and future accommodation.

Leeds Jewry

According to calculations by the Board of Deputies of British Jews using births, deaths and marriages, the current estimated Jewish population of Leeds is 8,000. As Chapter 4 explained, such estimates are necessarily prone to error, there being no method capable of providing an accurate figure acceptable to all members of the community. Despite the problems, however, there is little doubt that Leeds has followed the traditional pattern of regional British Jewry: a rapid increase in population from the 1880s, a peak in numbers in the 1950s, and considerable demographic decline since.

There have been Jews living in Leeds since at least the middle of the eighteenth century, and by the early years of the nineteenth century increased trading opportunities were attracting more. In 1825 the community had its own *shochet* (slaughterer of meat according to Jewish ritual), the first Jewish cemetery opened in 1840 and the first official marriage took place in 1842. Throughout the nineteenth century the population of Leeds Jewry increased, as Jews fled from poverty and persecution in Eastern Europe. Often the immigrants hoped to reach the United States, but remained in the United Kingdom because of a lack of funds. The usual journey was to travel from the Baltic states to the port of Hull, then across the country to Liverpool and then, ideally, to cross the Atlantic Ocean to the United States. However, many individuals and families ended up settling in the large industrial cities along that route: Leeds, Sheffield, Manchester and Liverpool. By 1877 the Jewish population of Leeds had reached 500 families, and in the following forty years numbers increased rapidly as the pogroms in Tsarist Russia intensified. By the 1950s the population of Leeds was estimated to include between 18,000 and 20,000 Jews.[2]

As the city's Jewish population grew in size, a variety of welfare organizations developed. In 1878 the Jewish Board of Guardians was founded, in 1905 the Herzl-Moser Jewish Hospital was opened (incorporated into the NHS system in 1948),[3] and in 1923 the Home for Aged Jews was built. Economically, Jews in Leeds were closely connected to the clothing industry, with Jewish immigrants providing a supply of cheap labour, as well as skilled tailors and business people. During the latter part of the nineteenth century, conditions in the sweatshops led to a series of general strikes by Leeds Jewish clothing workers. Throughout the twentieth century there was a steady rise in the overall economic status of the community, with more people entering the professions, and the steady migration of the population from inner-city areas, such as Leylands, to the suburbs of Moortown and Alwoodley, some of the wealthiest parts of the city.[4] Today, around 80 per cent of Leeds Jews live in the LS17 postcode, representing a remarkable concentration for a minority community with roots in the city dating back more than 200 years.

Despite the decline in the population, the community still remains strongly active, with facilities that include eight synagogues (seven Orthodox and one Reform), the voluntary-aided (state sector) Brodetsky primary school and nursery, a representative council and a range of Zionist, youth, educational, sporting and cultural groups. Leeds also has a large Jewish residential and nursing home, Donisthorpe Hall, and a day centre that caters for 100 people per day and delivers 200 kosher meals-on-wheels per week. There is also a large Jewish housing association (with over 400 units) that comes under the remit of the Leeds Jewish Welfare Board (LJWB). The LJWB is the centre of Jewish social services in the community, providing services particularly for older people, children and those with mental health needs. It employs over sixty people, including social workers trained to assess people's care needs and care staff to provide domiciliary services.

The Leeds Jewish Community Study

In July 2001 JPR launched the first component of its National Survey of British Jewry, with 5,000 questionnaires sent to households across the city of Leeds. The questionnaire comprised three sections (a general one for all respondents, one for the 'elderly or infirm', and one for households with children of school age), and included questions on schooling, health, social attitudes, culture, leisure, housing and migration. In designing a survey to gather information on the expectations and demands of Jews for Jewish services in the next decade, it was necessary to try to locate the 'potential market' for these services. There is, however, no complete communal list of Jews in Leeds, and so, primarily on the basis of distinctive Jewish names, questionnaires were sent to all households in which it was thought that there was at least one member who considered her/himself to be Jewish. This method erred on the side of inclusion, with the likelihood that many completely non-Jewish households received questionnaires (in addition to a certain percentage of Jewish households that may have been unintentionally omitted due to the difficulties in creating the list). Nevertheless, despite the difficulties of identifying Jews (see also Chapter 4), the survey represents by far the most comprehensive study of Leeds Jewry to date.[5]

This chapter provides information on those Leeds Jews who are aged 75 or over. Of the nearly 1,500 respondents to the questionnaire, around one-quarter were aged 75 or over. Such a large proportion of older respondents suggests that a very high percentage of this age group chose to answer the questionnaire, making the responses extremely reliable. Moreover, because it was a self-completion questionnaire with a large number of questions—there were 145 separate questions, a large number of which had many sub-components—it required high levels of motivation to complete and return. The high response rate therefore implies real concern among the population for the services provided by the organized Jewish community.

General and income characteristics

Of Leeds Jews aged 75 or over who returned completed questionnaires, 55 per cent were female. Over 60 per cent lived alone (compared with 21 per cent of Leeds Jews aged under 75, termed 'younger' from here on) and 54 per cent were widowed. Among the general UK population aged 75 and over, 48 per cent live alone, with the same percentage also widowed.[6] Older respondents in Leeds tend to have relatively low annual incomes: around a third had gross household incomes of less that £5,000, and only 23 per cent received more than £20,000 per year (compared with 71 per cent of younger Leeds Jews). This income distribution is not surprising given that the vast majority of this population are likely to be retired. Nevertheless, when asked about their pension provision, some 56 per cent stated that they had no arrangements other than the national pension scheme.

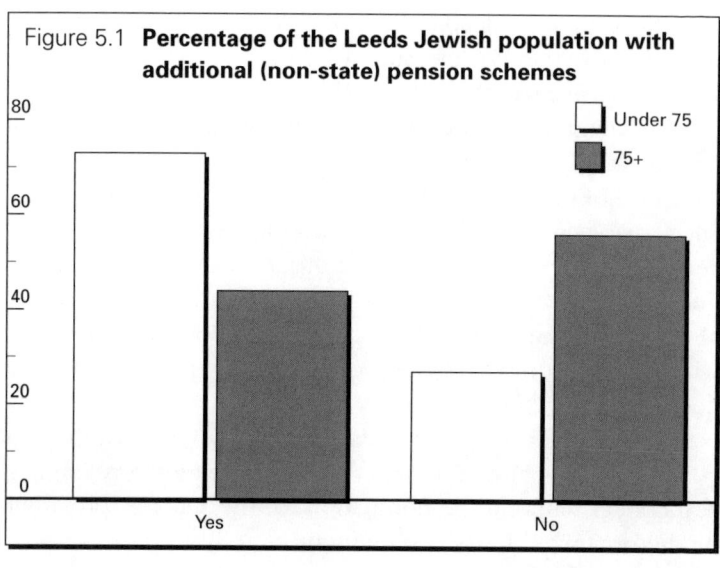

Figure 5.1 **Percentage of the Leeds Jewish population with additional (non-state) pension schemes**

Women were almost twice as likely not to have a private or occupational pension scheme than men: 38 per cent of older men had no additional pension scheme, compared with 74 per cent of older women (see Figure 5.1). Moreover, while the majority of those with additional pension schemes believed that these would be sufficient to allow them to maintain their previous lifestyle after retirement, a fifth did not (with men having more concerns about this than women). Those under 75 were much more likely to have an additional scheme than those who were older but, even so, a quarter of these respondents still did not have one. The age groups most unlikely to have such schemes were those under the age of 34, and those aged 70–4. The lack of pension provision by a large segment of the older Leeds Jewish population obviously has important implications for the ability of these individuals to pay for social care services. These figures suggest that the

Jewish voluntary sector will continue to have a major role to play for the foreseeable future.

Despite the relatively low incomes of older Jews and problems relating to lack of non-state pension provision, it is interesting to note how older people have incorporated new technologies. Twenty-nine per cent of older Jews said they used a mobile phone and 8 per cent a computer for e-mail purposes once a week or more often. It is also worth noting that 29 per cent of older people did some volunteering work during the previous year, compared with almost 50 per cent of Leeds Jews under the age of 75.

Jewish attitudes and practices

In terms of Jewish attitudes and beliefs, both older and younger Leeds Jews have remarkably high levels of 'traditional' attachments to Judaism. As Tables 5.1 and 5.2 show, the vast majority attend a traditional *seder* meal on Passover, and most buy only kosher meat (or else are vegetarians or vegans). Eighty-four per cent of older Jews (80 per cent of younger Jews) are also members of Orthodox synagogues.

Table 5.1 **Percentage of Leeds Jewish population that attends a *seder* meal on Passover**

	Percentage aged 75+ (n=376)	*Percentage aged under 75 (n=1,013)*
Never	6	5
Some years	13	8
Most years	9	9
Every year	72	78
Total	100	100

Table 5.2 **Type of meat bought by Leeds Jews**

	Percentage aged 75+ (n=373)	*Percentage aged under 75 (n=995)*
None (vegan or vegetarian)	18	8
Only meat from a kosher butcher	61	63
From an ordinary (non-kosher) butcher, but not pork products	16	20
From an ordinary (non-kosher) butcher including pork products	5	9
Total	100	100

Leeds Jews clearly have strong attachments to Judaism, but these appear to be more strongly influenced by 'tradition' (or arguably 'ethnicity') than by religious commitment *per se*. This is shown by the fact that only 7 per cent of older Jews (10 per cent of younger Jews) are fully Sabbath-observant, i.e. they never travel (by motorized transport) on this day. However, Leeds Jews are more likely to describe themselves as 'somewhat religious' than as 'somewhat secular' (see Figure 5.2).

When asked directly about their religious practice, the majority of Leeds Jews considered themselves to be 'traditional', with far lower percentages of strictly Orthodox and Progressive Jews than in the United Kingdom as a whole, as shown in the 1995 JPR survey of social and political attitudes of British Jewry (see Figure 5.3). The majority of the friends of older Leeds Jews are likely to be Jews, with almost three-quarters stating that more than half of their close friends are Jewish. Nevertheless, 37 per cent of those who answered the question concerning the extent to which they feel at ease with other Jews stated that they were uncomfortable or very

THE POTENTIAL SOCIAL CARE MARKETPLACE

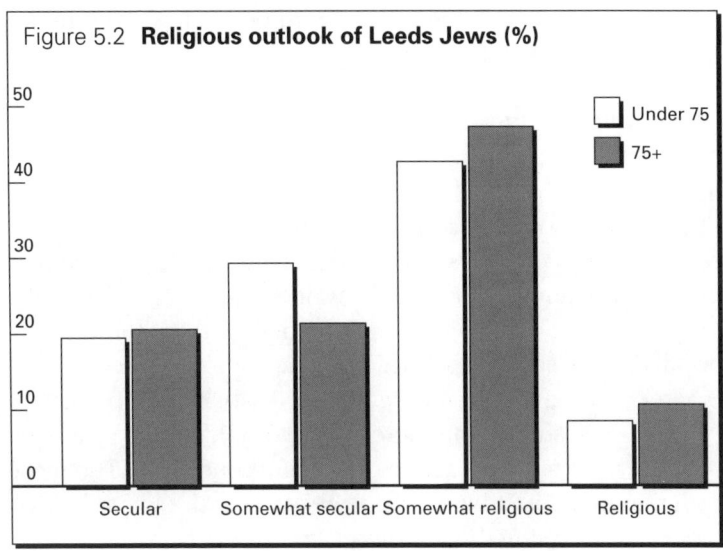

Figure 5.2 **Religious outlook of Leeds Jews (%)**

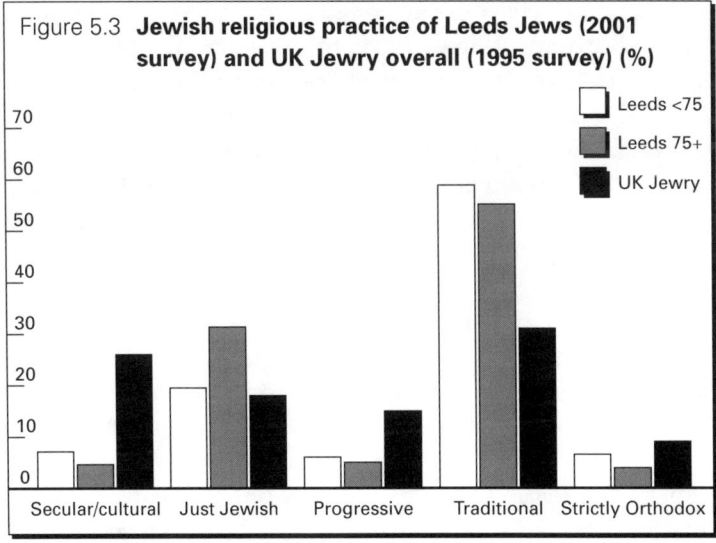

Figure 5.3 **Jewish religious practice of Leeds Jews (2001 survey) and UK Jewry overall (1995 survey) (%)**

uncomfortable with Haredi (ultra-Orthodox) Jews; the figure for younger Jews was 43 per cent.

The health of older Leeds Jews

As people become older, they are necessarily more likely to have specific medical conditions, which, for community planning purposes, it is important to ascertain. Over 70 per cent of older Leeds Jews have a long-standing illness, disability or infirmity, limiting the activities of 82 per cent of this sub-sample. These figures are slightly higher than for the UK population as a whole, of which 66 per cent of those aged 75 or over report a long-standing illness, disability or infirmity.[7]

Table 5.3 shows the percentage of older and younger Leeds Jews that have a range of specific conditions. The most common ailment is high blood pressure, with almost half of those 75+ reporting this condition, compared with only 23 per cent of younger Jews. One in five older respondents also stated that they have heart disease, whereas less than one in twelve of younger Jews have this condition. Among both groups there are notable levels of depression and anxiety, which should raise concern among communal planners.

Comparing the figures for Leeds with the UK as a whole (where there is comparable data), older Leeds Jews have higher self-reported rates of at least some ailments and medical conditions. According to the 1998 General Household Survey, 5 per cent of women and 4.3 per cent of men aged 75 or over report having asthma, compared with 12 per cent of older Leeds Jews.[8] In the Health Survey for England, 8.7 per cent of men and 6.6 per cent of women aged 75 or over stated that they had diabetes, whereas 9 per cent of older Leeds Jews reported this condition. The reported diabetes figure for the entire adult UK population was 3.3 per cent for men and 2.5 per cent for women, compared with 5

Table 5.3 **Medical conditions of Leeds Jews**

	Percentage aged 75+ with condition	Percentage under 75 with condition
High blood pressure	46	22
Heart disease	20	8
Asthma	12	13
Anxiety	10	7
Diabetes	9	5
Depression	6	8
Cancer	4	3
Parkinson's disease	1.8	<1.0
Drug dependency	1.5	<1.0
Crohn's disease	1.3	1.8
Alzheimer's disease/dementia	1.3	<1.0
An autoimmune disease (e.g. MS, lupus)	1.0	1.3
Eating disorder	<1.0	1.0

per cent for Leeds Jews under 75. However, it is important to draw distinctions between the *reporting* of conditions and actual *prevalence* rates. For example, there is known to be an under-reporting of diabetes with perhaps as many as one million people unaware that they have the condition. The higher rates of diabetes and asthma reported by the Leeds Jewish community may reflect higher numbers of Jews having these (and other) conditions, or it may be that they are simply more aware of their health than the general population.

Outside the Jewish community, it is known that members of ethnic minority communities are more likely to die from particular diseases and conditions than members of British society as a whole. For example, Asians have relatively high death rates from coronary heart disease, diabetes, tuberculosis and liver cancer, while migrants from the Caribbean are more likely to die from cardiovascular disease and strokes, liver cancer and complications resulting from diabetes. These higher rates may be linked to the psychosocial effects of migration and differences in diet.[9] With regard to the Jewish community, there are certainly grounds for further research to elucidate and explain the differences in the figures recorded for the Jewish and general populations.

Despite the rates of medical conditions, Jews are unlikely to drink or smoke. Only 6 per cent of older Jews smoke cigarettes (and 2 per cent cigars or pipes), and less than 2 per cent regularly drink more than the equivalent of two glasses of wine per day (14 units per week). For women aged 75 or over among the general UK population, 9 per cent smoke and 7 per cent consume more than 14 units of alcohol per week. For older men across the UK, 9 per cent smoke and 16 per cent regularly consume more than 21 units of alcohol per week (29 per cent consume 10 units or more).[10] In terms of exercise, 27 per cent of older Leeds Jews reported that they exercise regularly; the figure for younger Jews was 47 per cent.

Eighty-five per cent of older Jews had visited their local doctor (GP) in the three months prior to the survey, with a quarter doing so more than three times. For the general UK older population, 61 per cent visited their doctor in the previous three months.[11] More than half of the older respondents in Leeds (52 per cent) had visited a specialist during the same period and 15 per cent were on a waiting list for a surgical procedure; almost 4 per cent had been waiting for more than a year.

Mobility

Another key set of data needed for communal planners concerns the extent to which people are mobile and are able to carry out essential tasks within their own homes. This is important for ascertaining people's level of independence and thus calculating the extent to which domiciliary services are needed. It also provides an indication of future demand for long-term care facilities.

Table 5.4 **Ease with which older Leeds Jews can carry out essential tasks (%)**

	On my own, very easily	On my own, fairly easily	On my own, with difficulty	Only with help	Not at all
Getting to the toilet	65	23	11	<1.0	0
Dressing and undressing	63	27	7	3	0
Getting in and out of bed	60	30	9	<1.0	0
Bathing or showering	55	23	12	10	0
Making hot meals	51	23	10	5	11
Going shopping	41	21	11	16	11
Using public transport	41	18	11	4	26
Getting up and down stairs	39	30	22	5	4

Older Leeds respondents were, in the main, able to complete most household tasks on their own, although with varying degrees of difficulty. Indeed, they are more likely to manage on their own than the general UK population aged 75 or over: 27 per cent in Leeds cannot go shopping on their own, compared with 31 per cent in the UK; 9 per cent in Leeds cannot climb up and down stairs on their own, compared with 14 per cent; 3 per cent in Leeds need help dressing and undressing, whereas 8 per cent in the UK require this assistance; less than 1 per cent of Leeds Jews need assistance to get in and out of bed, while the figure for the UK is 3 per cent; and less than 1 per cent in Leeds cannot manage to get to the toilet on their own compared with 2 per cent for the UK.[12] The exception to this pattern is that 16 per cent of older Leeds Jews are unable to make a hot meal on their own compared with 11 per cent in the UK as a whole. These results show that, while a large majority in Leeds can cope fairly or very easily with most household tasks, a sizeable percentage still require assistance and even more struggle when it comes to completing activities outside the home.

In terms of domiciliary support, 14 per cent of older Leeds respondents received social services help with everyday household tasks, compared with 17 per cent of older people across the whole of the UK. Just under 30 per cent of older Leeds Jews stated that they have people to help them with everyday tasks, including the unpaid support of relatives and friends. Over two-thirds of older Leeds Jews requiring assistance had just a single helper, 14 per cent had two helpers and 17 per cent had three or more. Around 5 per cent of older Leeds Jews received meals-on-wheels at least two or three times a month (the same figure as for the UK generally) and 8 per cent had visited a day centre for older people (compared with 5 per cent for the UK).

The ease with which family and friends can visit older people is also extremely important in terms of the informal support systems available. As Chapter 2 noted, Jews have a long history of very strong family ties and a tradition of living in neighbourhoods with high Jewish concentrations. When asked how long it would take for the friend or family member who lives closest to them to visit (in case of an emergency), the vast majority (96 per cent) stated that they could arrive within one hour. Most older Jews live in Jewish neighbourhoods, with 86 per cent stating that they know of other Jews living on the same street as them, with two-thirds having Jewish next-door neighbours. Nevertheless, 13 per cent stated that friends and relatives visit them less than once a month (compared with 10 per cent for the UK as a whole), with 2.5 per cent stating that they never have such visitors (the same as for the UK).

Current and future accommodation

The final type of information that is needed for the assessment of present and future needs for services concerns people's current accommodation and their aspirations to move. Most older Jews in Leeds live in a flat or apartment (57 per cent), with most others living in single-family houses or bungalows. Three-quarters of respondents live in accommodation comprising two or three bedrooms, with a further 16 per cent living in homes with one bedroom. Over a fifth live in homes without central heating. Almost four-fifths of older Leeds Jews own their own homes, either outright, with the help of a mortgage or through a family trust. Among households across the United Kingdom containing at least one person aged 65 or over, 58 per cent are owner-occupied.[13]

Calculating individuals' moving plans is extremely important for the planning of services and, in particular, for deciding where to locate future community buildings. For older Leeds Jews, however, such an assessment is difficult to make. When asked about their plans to move residence over the next few years, 9 per cent expected to move in the next ten years, 6 per cent believed they would stay where they were, and the remainder (85 per cent) did not know. Nevertheless, when it comes to moves to institutional care homes, what is most significant is the residential location of the *families* of older people. Eight per cent of younger Leeds Jews expected to move within the next two years, and 29 per cent expected to move within the next ten years. Of the very small numbers (4 per cent) who stated they were actively searching for a new home, 54 per cent said they were looking in the Alwoodley area, 35 per cent elsewhere in the LS17 postal district, 16 per cent elsewhere in Leeds, and 7 per cent in London and the South-east.[14] The small number of responses limits the reliability of the answers to this question, but does suggest that, in the short term at least, most Jewish householders who are going to move will stay in Alwoodley and the LS17 area.

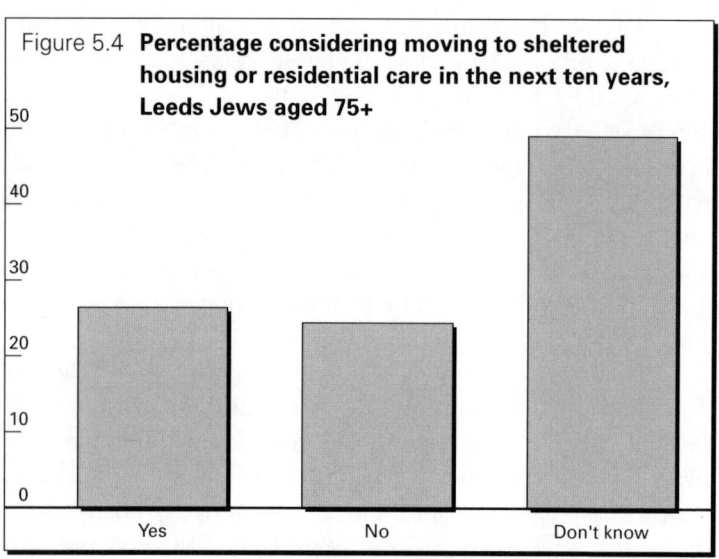

Figure 5.4 **Percentage considering moving to sheltered housing or residential care in the next ten years, Leeds Jews aged 75+**

The questionnaire also asked older people whether or not they would consider moving to sheltered housing or residential care in the next ten years. Over half of respondents answered 'don't know', a quarter 'no', with the remaining 24 per cent answering 'yes' (see Figure 5.4). These responses suggest that, while most older people are unwilling or unable to think about their medium- or long-term accommodation needs, there is a sizeable population that is thinking seriously about making use of sheltered housing or long-term institutional care.

Conclusions

The findings from the Leeds component of the National Survey of British Jewry are obviously of major relevance to that city's communal planners. However, they are also likely to resonate with the experiences of other large regional Jewish centres and indeed with other ethnic minority communities across the United Kingdom. The survey paints a picture of a community that has strong attachments to Judaism, although these are more likely to be due to social and cultural (or 'ethnic') factors, than to strong religious beliefs. Most older Leeds Jews have a majority of friends who are Jewish, but for many this does not include Haredi (ultra-Orthodox) Jews, whom they clearly see as different and 'other'.

The older Leeds Jewish population has, unsurprisingly, higher rates of medical conditions than younger Jews, with almost half reporting high blood pressure and a fifth having heart disease. The community reports higher rates of diabetes and asthma (and potentially of other conditions too) than the United Kingdom as a whole, reflecting either higher prevalence rates or an increased health awareness among the population. These issues require urgent further research.

A sizeable percentage of the older Leeds Jewish community have mobility problems, with, for example, 10 per cent needing help with bathing or showering and a quarter of respondents stating that they cannot use public transport at all. Older Leeds Jews report slightly higher rates of long-standing illnesses, disabilities or infirmities than older people generally, although they are more likely to be able to manage essential tasks on their own (except for being able to prepare a hot meal for themselves).

In terms of their incomes and assets—and hence their ability to pay for social care services—a large proportion have relatively low annual incomes (although most are likely to be retired). Over half of older Jews rely only on the state pension—challenging the stereotype of Jews as universally well off and thus able to 'look after their own'—with women far less likely to have an additional scheme than men. Nevertheless, most older Jews live in their own home, which they are likely to own outright or with a mortgage. When asked about their accommodation plans, very few are looking to move in the next few years, although one-quarter of Jews aged 75 or over would consider moving to sheltered housing or to a care home in the next ten years.

Notes

1 A forthcoming JPR report by Stanley Waterman will provide a further and more complete analysis of the Leeds Jewish population.
2 Ernest Krausz, *Leeds Jewry: Its History and Social Structure* (Cambridge: Jewish Historical Society of England 1964).
3 Note that the NHS incorporated all the old British Jewish hospitals in 1948, the reason why none of these facilities exist today.
4 Krausz.
5 For a full discussion of the methodology behind the survey, see the forthcoming report by Waterman. See also Stanley Waterman and Barry Kosmin, 'Mapping an unenumerated ethnic population: Jews in London', *Ethnic and Racial Studies*, vol. 9, 1986, 484–501, and Valins, 'Identity, Space and Boundaries'.
6 Office for National Statistics.

7   Ibid.
8   Ibid.
9   Kenneth Blakemore and Margaret Boneham, *Age, Race and Ethnicity: A Comparative Approach* (Buckingham: Open University Press 1994). See also Moyra Sidell, *Health in Old Age: Myth, Mystery and Management* (Buckingham: Open University Press 1995). For an interesting historical perspective on apparent differences in rates of diseases and medical conditions between Jews and the wider society, see the special issue of *Patterns of Prejudice* on 'The new genetics and the old eugenics: the ghost in the machine', especially Sander L. Gilman, 'Private knowledge', *Patterns of Prejudice*, vol. 36, no. 1, 2002, 5–16, and Klaus Hödl, 'The black body and the Jewish body: a comparison of medical images', *Patterns of Prejudice*, vol. 36, no. 1, 2002, 17–34.
10 Department of Health, 'Health survey for England'.
11 Eileen Goddard and David Savage, *People Aged 65 and Over: A Study Carried Out on Behalf of the Department of Health as Part of the 1991 General Household Survey* (London: HMSO 1994).
12 UK figures from Goddard and Savage.
13 UK figures from Goddard and Savage.
14 Note that percentages here do not add up to 100, because people may be looking in more than one area.

6 Institutional care: choosing a care home

The first half of this book concentrated on demographic trends, the broad provision of social care services within the Jewish community and in the United Kingdom, and current and potential use of social care services. The second half focuses on one particular aspect of long-term care provision: Jewish residential and nursing home care. As Chapter 3 reported, institutional care is the single largest component of social care expenditure for older people. Over the last decade millions of pounds of Jewish communal money have been spent on building new care homes and updating older facilities. This continues more than 150 years of investment by the community in bricks-and-mortar institutions designed to care for older people within a culturally and religiously sensitive environment. These institutions account for tens of millions of pounds each year in running costs, with funds coming from local authorities and central government, as well as considerable contributions from individual residents, either through their pension schemes, income earned or the sale of assets such as their homes. However, gaps in the funding supplied by local authorities for the running of these institutions means that many care homes are using their reserves to subsidize the shortfalls (see Chapter 8).

Despite the remarkable levels of communal financial investment, there have been very few studies of institutional care provided by the Jewish community. Indeed, the needs of ethnic minority older people in general have been low on the policy and research agenda.[1] To help address this deficit this chapter explores how Jews go about choosing a care home for themselves and their relatives, and the factors that are important in their decision-making. The first part examines the process of choosing a care home, and discusses some of the barriers and the challenges involved. The second part outlines some of the key factors involved in choosing a care home, particularly issues relating to geographical location, environment and standards, and Jewish ethos. The chapter is based on qualitative interviews with Jewish families across the United Kingdom who have relatives in care homes, as well as older people themselves. Because of the increasing frailties of those entering institutional care, the key decision-makers are typically the relatives of older people, rather than the prospective residents.

The process of choosing a care home

Under the 1990 National Health Service and Community Act, local authorities are required to allow older people to choose their own care home, although within certain funding and suitability limitations. For Jewish 'clients' needing residential or nursing home care, there are potential choices to be made involving such issues as the geographical proximity of the institution, its ethos, the costs involved, and the social environment and standards. Nevertheless, there are also a series of barriers, including the availability of places, demands that residents must be Jewish (relevant for mixed marriage couples), government funding limitations and geographical location. In reality, choice may be more myth than reality, particularly for those wanting care within a specifically Jewish facility (see Figure 6.1). Moreover, the actual process of choosing a care home can be extremely distressing, both for older people themselves and for their close relatives who are increasingly the prime decision-makers.

CHOOSING A CARE HOME

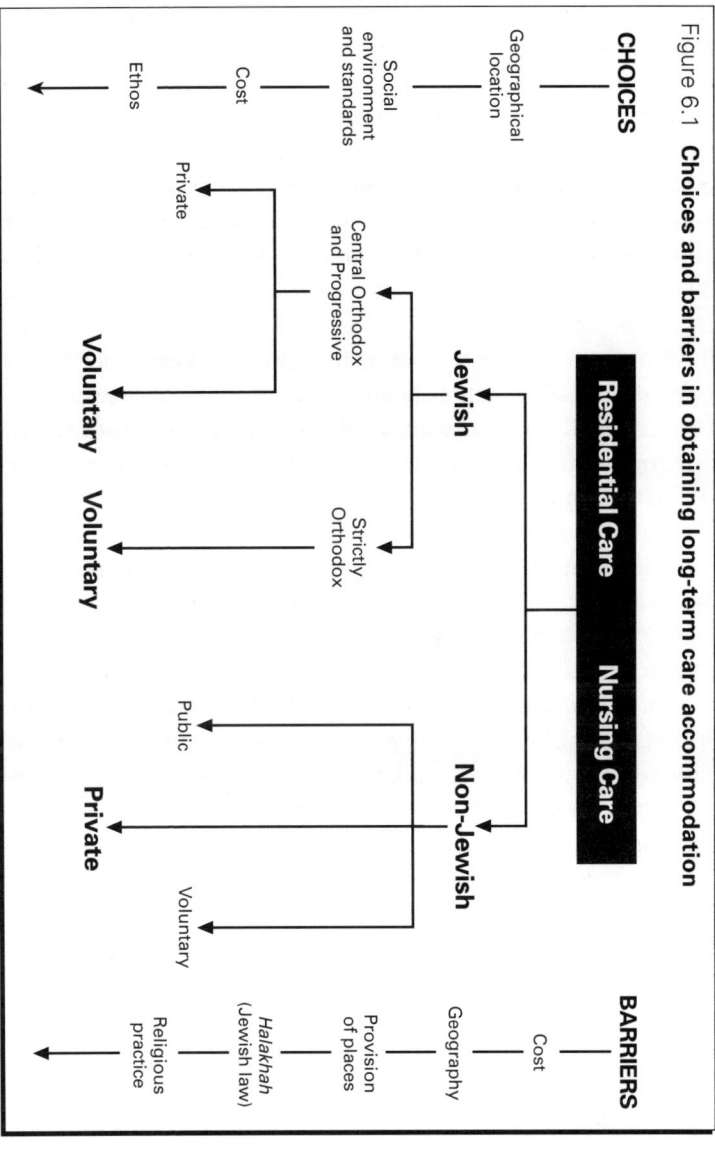

Figure 6.1 **Choices and barriers in obtaining long-term care accommodation**

Despite the ideals of a consumerist approach to care propagated by successive governments, choosing a residential or nursing home does not often take place within a calm and reflective environment in which older people and their families can look at different facilities and make informed choices at their leisure. Rather, care homes are often chosen over a relatively short period of time, because of, for example, a sudden decline in the health of a family member who may have experienced a stroke, accident or illness. Decisions may be made at a time of crisis, with a great deal of information needing to be absorbed at a moment when loved ones, who may have been independent all their lives, suddenly face the prospect of moving to an institutional environment. Indeed, across the United Kingdom 63 per cent of older people permanently entering nursing home care, and around 43 per cent of those entering residential homes, come directly from hospital.[2] Accordingly, several interviewees spoke of the 'trauma of decision-making': 'at the time we only had a few days to find her a place, we had to become an expert in a very short space of time'; 'the whole thing was traumatic and terrible'; 'it's a very difficult time, I'm not sure when making the decision if I was really on the ball, I really didn't know what to ask'. Another interviewee spoke of how this was a time of shock, as the reversal of the parent–child relationship became clear:

> It used to be the parent looking after the child, and now it's the child looking after the parent and the role is reversed. You never see yourself in that situation. It's always the women who feel the brunt of it.

Even when the need for residential or nursing care is more predictable, as would be the case when individuals are showing increasing symptoms of Alzheimer's disease or other progressive forms of dementia, accepting and planning for institutional care is never easy.

> It is immensely difficult [to choose a care home]. It is difficult to know what to look for, how to check standards are high, how to judge kindness and sensitivity, how to know whether enough nursing support will be offered. Equally, it is hard to understand how the system works, who funds what, what an older person is entitled to, and why there are sometimes problems with discharge from hospital. Through all this, the person doing the choosing is often not the person who is going to live in the care home. One is choosing for someone else—often for someone vulnerable, possibly confused, and perhaps where a crisis has occurred that makes living at home no longer viable. The sense of responsibility is considerable, and the difficulties may be substantial.[3]

In most circumstances, the decision as to whether or not an older person is to move to a care home—or, indeed, to receive other forms of care—is taken in conjunction with National Health Service (NHS) and/or social service professionals. Within a hospital, doctors, nurses, physiotherapists and occupational therapists help to co-ordinate the move to a care home. However, it is the local authority (usually through a designated care manager) that specifically arranges for care in a home, and also pays for those who need financial help. Most of the major centres of Jewish population have specific Jewish social service agencies that help with individual client needs and put the case for long-term care funding to the local authority. In London and the South-east of England, for example, Jewish Care runs a dedicated Social Work Help Desk that provides advice and information, as well as social workers trained in the specific needs of Jewish people. In Glasgow, Jewish Care Scotland is able to make statutory assessments of clients' needs (and funding requirements) for long-term care through local authority social workers based at its centre in Giffnock.

Assistance in the decision-making process can also be obtained via publications, such as the King's Fund guide to choosing a care home, *Home from Home*, the Department of Health information leaflet *Moving into a Care Home*, and advice from national charities such as Help the Aged and Age Concern.[4] Care homes also produce brochures advertising their services, and all will have inspection reports that are available for public consultation (although these are often available in public facilities such as libraries, rather than easily accessible in individual homes). Several service providers spoke of being relatively content with the current system, with one questioning how far agencies should really go in helping people choose between different organizations.

> The Jewish community is a very sophisticated community of askers. People will move heaven and earth to get their parent into a home. People develop great skills very quickly in phoning the various institutions and they will pick which is the best deal for them, and the more aggravated they get about the waiting lists that one organization says it has, they'll go to another one if they can move there quicker and get the funding. There's no brand loyalty (social service professional).

> I would argue, speaking personally, that in a sense it's like when you're making those personal decisions

> about which car to buy, which house to buy. There are documents available to you, to help you make your choice (social service professional).

Service users sometimes—though certainly not always—expressed more concerns. For some, particularly those in regional communities, the choice was a relatively simply one, between attending a Jewish voluntary sector home (in many Jewish communities there is only one) or a private facility that may or may not specifically cater for Jewish needs. In Greater London there are many more options, because of the greater number and range of facilities.

There are nineteen Jewish voluntary sector homes within the Greater London boundaries, three elsewhere in the Southeast of England, and many more private facilities (see Chapter 4). These homes vary in size, geographical location (although most are clustered around the south of Barnet), ethos and date of construction. Some homes in the capital are struggling to fill their places, but others, especially those with the latest facilities or with particularly good reputations, have waiting lists. Several interviewees expressed frustration that the preferred home for their relatives was full, and that they were faced with the choice of either waiting for a vacancy—'it's dead men's shoes, waiting for someone to die before others can move in'—or else settling for a second or third choice. Where homes are effectively 'rationing' places due to high demand, choices may be limited to less popular facilities.

One interviewee compared the process of choosing a care home with trying to find a school place for one's child: some homes are, similar to the best schools, often over-subscribed. The key difference, however, is that the decision to move to a care home may have to be made in a fraction of the time and at a moment of crisis. Some interviewees spoke of using *protectsia* to try to get a place at their preferred home, i.e. using contacts in agencies and individual homes to put in a 'good word' and thus speed the process along. Many Jewish voluntary sector homes operate by providing places according to levels of assessed need, so that people with the most pressing needs will be accepted before those considered less urgent, even if the latter have been waiting longer.

A number of interviewees spoke of how they chose their preferred home via 'word-of-mouth' or 'some sort of instinct'. Brochures were often not considered especially useful—'they're awful, not informative at all' (relative of a care home resident)—while inspection reports are typically written in a language designed for care home managers, rather than for service users. Potential clients can also visit homes to experience the 'feel' of the place, although in facilities that are over-subscribed this may not be possible. Moreover, even when a person gains a place in a specific home, service users may—depending on their 'means test'—have to face the difficulty of understanding and coping with the financial realities of paying for care.

The majority of older people living in Jewish voluntary sector homes are funded by local authorities, which pay (ideally, at least: see Chapter 8) for the costs of care, leaving residents with just a small amount of 'pocket money' for personal use, as well as any assets that fall below the minimum threshold. Those with assets above £18,500 have to pay the full costs of institutional care (see Chapter 3). Several interviewees whose older relatives were liable for the full costs of care argued that they would have liked more financial advice to help them plan for future needs. One of the most strident concerns came from an interviewee who was sharply critical of how one particular care home dealt with the financial affairs of his relative. He believed the manager had tried to 'con' him into signing over his relative's home as a once-only payment that would cover all future costs. At a vulnerable time when this interviewee's relative had to move to institutional care, he believed the home was trying to take advantage of him. He argued that he 'received no [independent] help or guidance', and believed that this was because they were paying for care privately. In fact, advice and assistance could have been provided by the local Jewish social services, but a lack of knowledge about how the system works and who to turn to in times of need prevented him from accessing this help. This need to improve communication and the information available to service users is discussed in Chapter 9.

Despite the difficulties of, and the barriers to, choosing among individual care homes in some parts of London, interviewees with relatives in Jewish residential and nursing homes had fairly clear ideas about why they chose one particular home over another. The key factors in the decision-making process were *geographical location, social environment and standards* and *Jewish ethos.*

Key factors in choosing a care home

Geographical location

For most service users, the 'over-riding' factor in their choice of care homes appears to be geographical location. What seems to matter most, however, is not the residential location of older people themselves, but rather that of their close family. As one relative explained: 'we had to find somewhere that had a vacancy, but also somewhere close to where I live, really how easy it would be for me to visit him or bring him a meal ... this was a really big factor for me.'

The traditional pattern of migration for Jewish (particularly Ashkenazi) communities in the United Kingdom (and indeed elsewhere in Europe) has been to move from inner-city areas—where they first settled during the nineteenth century—to the suburbs.[5] This migration reflects the rising socio-economic status of Jews, from being a poor immigrant community 100 years ago to one that is now a settled component of British society. In Greater London, however, this traditional out-migration has been compromised by the seemingly increasing desire among younger people to live closer to the centres of cities, from which commuting times are much less and the quality of life therefore perceived to be greater. The extent to which this phenomenon is occurring, and the age groups of those most likely to move, is something that is being investigated by JPR's National Survey of British Jewry (see Preface). Moreover, the rapid growth in the number of strictly Orthodox Jews, who often settle in those inner-city locations where rents and property values are cheaper, is another important counter to processes of suburbanization.[6]

Residential and nursing homes are extremely expensive constructions, with new facilities costing millions of pounds. However, care homes are not 'footloose' in that, once money has been invested in a bricks-and-mortar construction in a specific place, they cannot relocate without considerable expense; hence the importance of choosing the best location for facilities. In London, all of the recently constructed facilities have been in the borough of Barnet, with the exception of the Agudas Israel facility in Hackney, catering for strictly Orthodox communities. Homes in the South-east of England that were located in areas where Jews are no longer living have gradually been closed down, although there are still some exceptions to this rule, notably the large Nightingale House in Clapham, South London. Around three-quarters of residents of Nightingale House had formerly lived in North London, but have chosen to live there either because of its reputation as one of the best homes in the country or because of some other connection with the home. Those associated with the home argued that it is probably in the wrong location given the concentration of Jews in North-west London, although there are still around 19,000 Jews south of the River Thames and in North Kent and North Surrey (see Chapter 4). Nonetheless, the home remains popular. In this sense, the quality and reputation of a facility is able, at least in part, to counter the problems of geographical location. This said, several interviewees argued that they would seriously have considered Nightingale House but for the fact that the bus service designed to bring people to it from North London only operates once a week.

Outside London, only Manchester has a choice of voluntary sector Jewish homes.[7] Travelling times in Manchester are far shorter than in the capital, allowing people a greater choice in facilities, although in the south of the city (which has fewer Jews than the north) there is again only one facility, the Morris Feinmann care home. One of the other homes is the newly opened Beenstock facility in Broughton Park, which caters for strictly Orthodox Jews. Accordingly, most older Jews requiring long-term care effectively have a choice of only one or two voluntary sector homes, with the majority opting for the large Heathlands home. Elsewhere in regional Jewish communities there is typically only one Jewish home. The question for these communities concerns what kind of provision will be available for older Jews, if the decline in these populations continues (and there is no indication to suggest otherwise). Will they choose (or be able) to move to larger communities with a more sustainable Jewish infrastructure?

Social environment and standards

Alongside the geographical practicalities of where homes are located and the ease with which people can visit their relatives, a second crucial factor in the decision-making process is the environment of the home and the (perceived) standards of care. The thirty-six Jewish voluntary sector homes and the dozens of private facilities that cater for Jews vary in their atmosphere and in the quality of facilities offered. Care homes vary from those that are fairly small and seek to provide a 'family' type of atmosphere, to larger ones aiming for a 'hotel' environment. Some interviewees spoke of certain homes being too large and therefore impersonal. Others considered that only larger homes with both residential and nursing options available were suitable. These institutions are able to cater for the growing needs of family members, so that they would not have to move to a new care home if/when their condition deteriorates.

Beyond the question of size, interviewees also had dramatically different opinions about care homes. Some homes had national reputations for excellence, with modern en-suite facilities, beautiful décor, cultural facilities and rooms with the latest facilities. Standards of facilities are constantly rising, with homes having to adapt because of both direct consumer pressure and government legislation (Chapter 3).

> I would never contemplate going into a home without an en-suite toilet and shower—I wouldn't go to a hotel that didn't have that, so why should I go to a residential home? I would like to think I could go upstairs to my room in the afternoon and switch on my television, therefore I would expect to have a TV point built in, I would expect to have a telephone built in so I can keep in touch with my family, and a

> refrigerator built in, because most people who go into homes have things brought into them by their children ... *I always said that if I don't want to go there myself or my parents, there's something wrong with the place* (social service professional).

Voluntary and private sector care homes catering for Jews have spent millions of pounds in recent years on new facilities, but standards of care across the sector are by no means uniform.

> We visited [one particular] house, but it looked run-down, people just sitting there doing nothing. It was under-funded and needed a facelift. It reminded me of an institution, it felt like people were being processed. There was no feeling of personality or individuality, no feeling of life or lustre—a place where you're going to die (relative of care home resident).

> Some of the homes that we saw are not inviting, they look like old institutional homes, there's long corridors, there's creamy beige paint, the chairs are the plastic wing chairs all the way round the perimeter of the rooms, and there's nothing inviting about them (relative of care home resident).

Criticisms of some care homes included residents 'sitting in chairs like dead bodies' around the perimeter of lounges, urine smells in the rooms and alert residents feeling depressed at having to mix with people suffering from dementia. In any case, relatives of people living in care homes tended to form fairly quick impressions of care homes, in which the appearance of facilities—as well as the residents themselves—was a key factor. The strengths and weaknesses of life in Jewish voluntary sector care homes are discussed in the following chapter.

Jewish ethos

A third key factor that is crucial for older Jewish people and their families in choosing a care home is Jewish ethos. For strictly Orthodox Jews having a home that is fully kosher and that is observant of all the rules of the Sabbath is a religious requirement. As such, the strictly Orthodox communities in Stamford Hill, London and Broughton Park, Manchester have constructed two homes specifically designed for these communities. The homes are fitted with electronic devices to ensure that the Sabbath rules are not broken, for example by having lifts that do not require buttons to be pressed, lights that are on automatic timers and food that is *glatt* kosher.[8] All other Jewish voluntary sector homes also adopt many Orthodox requirements. All the food that is cooked will be kosher (although not *glatt* kosher), so that there will be, for example, separate kitchens for the cooking of meat and dairy dishes (in Jewish law it is forbidden to mix these). The Sabbath will be observed as far as possible as a rest day with communal televisions not turned on and music not played; individuals in their own rooms can usually do whatever they please, although bringing in non-kosher food is discouraged. The many Jewish festivals and holy days will be observed in these homes, for example by not eating leaven during the eight days of Passover, by the blowing of the *shofar* (ram's horn) on the high holy days of the Jewish New Year and the Day of Atonement, or by trying to create a carnival atmosphere on Purim (which commemorates a foiled plot to destroy the Jews living in ancient Persia). Larger Jewish homes are also likely to have their own synagogues for use by residents and members of the wider community. Many Jews have grown up with and practised these religious and cultural aspects of Judaism all their lives and, as such, they are fundamental to what they (or their relatives) are looking for in a home. Nevertheless, maintaining such a Jewish atmosphere is difficult given that almost all the members of staff are non-Jewish (see Chapter 8). Interviewees were certainly aware of a 'cultural gap' between staff and residents, and indeed some expressed prejudiced attitudes: a problem that may have to be addressed by care home managers, especially given the difficulties of staff recruitment and retention.

Many Jews are not religious, and may in fact have had relatively little active involvement in Jewish ways of life before entering a care home. Nevertheless, for many of these people moving to a specifically Jewish residential or nursing home is also really important as they wish to 'return to what they know' and want to spend the latter part of their lives with other Jews.

> Sometimes it's obvious, they want kosher food, access to a synagogue etc. etc., but in other cases kosher food is irrelevant, access to a synagogue is irrelevant, so one can only conclude that it's cultural reasons. Somehow they feel they can relax more and feel more comfortable with people who come from a similar background (care home manager).

> There are still lots and lots of people who have been brought up in a Jewish environment, who have been used, if not exclusively, then certainly largely to a Jewish environment, where most of their friends are Jewish, where they've eaten kosher food, Jewish-style food. As long as there is a demand for that we want

> to provide it, and there clearly is a demand (care
> home manager).

One resident argued that when choosing a care home he never even considered a non-Jewish facility: 'it would be like denying my past.' He argued that the residents of a Jewish home 'aren't strangers, they understand what I'm talking about, I don't need to explain things'. For him, the other residents were somehow the same as he, so that even if he had thought that a non-Jewish facility had better standards of care, he would still have only considered a Jewish institution. Such residents are more likely to have a shared sense of humour, and perhaps to have followed similar professions. This resident, for example, had worked in the clothing industry—known in Yiddish as the *shmatter* (or 'rag') trade—which was very common among Jewish immigrants and their descendents.

> It's the difference between visiting the Vatican—which
> I have, and I love the art there—and my local *shul*
> [synagogue]. It's like wearing a shoe that fits well.
> Why would I want to wear a shoe that doesn't fit
> properly? I like my shoes to be comfortable (care
> home resident).

This particular resident was also a Holocaust survivor, and those who have directly or indirectly experienced the horrors of state-sanctioned antisemitism are especially likely to want to live in a Jewish environment at the end of their days. In this way the Otto Schiff Housing Association (which has recently merged with Jewish Care) was established to care for the Jewish refugees from Nazi persecution, with its care homes in North London designed to be sensitive to the needs of these people (staff, for example, do not wear uniforms to try to lessen the home's institutional ambience). Numbers of Holocaust survivors are inevitably declining more than half a century after the concentration camps were liberated. Nevertheless, even those who have always lived in this country sometimes grew up in the shadow of virulent antisemitism, especially during the 1930s when Sir Oswald Mosley's British Union of Fascists failed in its attempts to march through Cable Street in the Jewish East End of London.[9]

A number of interviewees pointed out that a key attraction of a Jewish home was the food, often not so much that it was kosher, but that it was 'Jewish'. One interviewee described how, although her father 'hated being in the home', he liked the 'nice German Jewish food, the way he was used to'. For her, there could be no thought of placing him in a care home with 'English' food: 'the sad thing about homes is that meals become the highlight of the day, hence the importance of food.' One service provider questioned why residents had to be served the traditional foods of chopped liver, chicken soup, roast chicken and potatoes every Friday night. As an experiment he decided to change the menu, but this proved extremely unpopular: 'I thought I was going to be lynched!' Nonetheless, people's ideas of what constitutes Jewish food vary.

> One of the single biggest issues in a home like this is food, as you can imagine. A lot of residents will say to us, there's not enough traditional *heimishe* [homely, traditional Jewish] food here, why can't we have more *heimishe* Jewish food? A lot of other residents will turn round to us and say, who do you think we are, peasants? Why can't we have proper food? (care home manager).

Conclusions

As Chapter 4 showed, the majority of Jews entering long-term residential or nursing care choose to live in either a Jewish voluntary sector care home or in private facilities that specifically cater for their needs. The 'Jewish' aspects of care are clearly very important to their choice of institution; the other key factors are the proximity of facilities to relatives and the perception of social environment and standards. Nevertheless, the principle of choice (enshrined in legislation) is sometimes more myth than reality. There are several barriers to entering the care home of a person's choice, including the difficulties of obtaining local authority funding and waiting lists for the most popular facilities. Moreover, choosing a care home is often done at a time of crisis, and there are difficulties in obtaining and absorbing large amounts of crucial information in a sometimes very short period of time.

Notes

1 Blakemore and Boneham; Sarah Harper, 'Ageing update: ageing 2000—questions for the 21st century', *Ageing and Society*, vol. 20, 2000, 111–22; Naina Patel, 'Black and minority ethnic elderly: perspectives on long-term care', in Royal Commission on Long Term Care, Research Volume 1.
2 Department of Health, *National Service Framework*, 46. See also Nardi Steverink, 'When and why frail elderly people give up independent living: The Netherlands as an example', *Ageing and Society*, vol. 21, 2001, 45–69.
3 Julia Neuberger, 'Foreword', in Alison Turnbull (ed.), *Home from Home: Your Guide to Choosing a Care Home* (London: King's Fund 1998), ix.

4 Turnbull (ed.); Department of Health, *Moving into a Care Home*.
5 Ashkenazi Jews are of Eastern European origin; Sephardi Jews are those of Middle Eastern, Mediterranean or North African origins.
6 Note, however, that even in inner-city locations such as Hackney in North London where many strictly Orthodox Jews live, house prices and rents have increased rapidly over recent years, posing major challenges to the community: see Christine Holman, *Orthodox Jewish Housing Need in Stamford Hill* (London: Agudas Israel Housing Association 2001).
7 Note that Glasgow has two voluntary sector care homes. These are, however, run by one organization and have developed as the old home, Newark Lodge, is replaced by two new facilities that are half its size.
8 *Glatt* kosher means that food is checked by religious authorities to a 'higher' and more exacting standard that 'ordinary' kosher food.
9 See Alderman.

7 Institutional care: living in a Jewish voluntary sector care home

Decisions regarding the future provision of services for older people are often made on the basis of predictions of demographic trends, financial costings, the views of social care professionals and, occasionally, the friends and relatives of those in long-term care settings. Nevertheless, older people themselves are often unrepresented in such discussions, and planners—and indeed the public more generally—may have little actual sense of what it is like to live in an institutional care setting. Accordingly, services are frequently provided *to* older people, rather than *with* older people and their families. To help address this problem this chapter describes life in residential and nursing homes, and then outlines some of the strengths and weaknesses of current provision.

The first part of the chapter provides three day-in-the-life case-studies of older people: first, 'Rose' who lives in a large residential care home; second, 'Alfred' who resides in an elderly mentally infirm (EMI) unit of a small residential home; and third, 'Miriam' who is in a medium-sized nursing home. These case-studies are based on interviews and conversations with older people living in care homes and the staff who look after them. Each is an *amalgam* of the experiences of different residents, with the actual names of those spoken to, and indeed the care homes visited, changed so as to protect anonymity and confidentiality. The studies are intended to enable those who have little or no experiences of care homes to understand better the lifestyles and routines of individuals living in them. However, it is important to recognize that there are wide variations in the standards, facilities and practices of different homes, although elements of institutionalized routines discussed in each case-study were common to all of the places visited.

The second part of the chapter discusses the implications of these case-studies, which vividly demonstrate many of the strengths and weaknesses of current institutional provision. This discussion is based on interviews with care home managers, social service professionals, nursing and care staff, older people living in care homes, relatives of people living in care homes, and visits to over a dozen homes across Britain. In many ways Jewish residential and nursing homes represent the best in institutional care in terms of the range of facilities provided, the commitment of staff and the input of volunteers. Nevertheless, there are still fundamental problems in the models of institutional care that present major challenges to social care providers seeking to develop and modernize their services.

A day in the life of Jewish residential and nursing clients

Case-study 1: 'Rose'

Rose has lived at Meadow Lodge residential home for eighteen months. Her husband died five years ago from oesophageal cancer, and for the following three-and-a-half years she lived alone in her home, with increasing levels of domiciliary support and kosher meals-on-wheels delivered by a local Jewish charity. She has two children, a son who lives in the United States and a daughter who lives close to her old home in North-west London. In January 2000 Rose had an accident outside her home and broke her arm. After a period in hospital, her daughter persuaded her to move to a care home, because her increasing levels of physical frailty meant that she could no longer look after herself without very high levels of support. Rose was also very lonely living at home.

Meadow Lodge is a large, well-established voluntary sector home with over 100 residents and it caters exclusively for Jewish residents. It has recently undergone a major conversion so that all rooms are now en-suite (toilet, basin and shower), and prepared to the same standard, with 14 square metres of space containing a bed, wardrobe, chest of drawers and large writing desk. Rose has decorated her room with photographs of her family and some of her favourite paintings. She also has her own television, telephone and a portable radio. The care home has a good reputation and, unlike one or two other homes she visited before she arrived here, there is no smell of urine; the place is always kept very clean.

7.30 a.m. Rose has been awake for the past hour. She has arthritis and it has been causing her pain recently. Most of the other residents are also already awake by the time the night staff 'hand over' their reports to the incoming day staff. Rose is able partially to dress herself, but she cannot put on her socks and shoes without the assistance of care staff.

8–9 a.m. At five minutes before 8 o'clock Rose arrives for breakfast. Although the home is quite large, residents are divided according to the floor on which they live, which is where all meals are provided. Breakfast is served between 8 and 9 a.m., although there is invariably a queue of residents waiting outside before it is served. At 8 o'clock the lights in the dining room are turned on and everyone makes their way to their table. Although individuals can in theory sit where they like, the practice is that everyone has their own table and they share all their meals with the same people. Rose shares a table with three other women, all of whom are physically frail but mentally active, although at most of the other tables residents show signs of greater mental frailty. The care home has a separate wing for those suffering from severe dementia, but many others also have cognitive functioning problems. Rose hates having to eat in the dining room with people who are confused; it makes her feel old and reminds her that she is now living in an institution.

The tables are all set before the residents arrive, and breakfast is brought to them. Some residents choose to have meals brought to them in their own rooms. If residents do not arrive by 9 a.m. they miss breakfast, although the floor does have a small kitchenette with a kettle and a fridge so that they can make themselves a cup of tea. Residents all dress for breakfast and indeed for all meals. A couple of months ago a new resident arrived for breakfast in his pyjamas and dressing gown, and was shouted at by those who had been living in the home much longer: 'what do you think this is, your home?' Residents are extremely quick to show newcomers 'the ropes' and to make clear what are the 'proper' ways of behaving. Breakfast is also the time when Rose receives her morning medicines.

9–10 a.m. After breakfast, Rose returns to her room and awaits the arrival of care staff who are going to help her bathe. Bathing in the home usually takes place twice a week. Rose has a shower in her room, but she does not make use of it because she is worried about falling, and, in any case, when she was living in her own home she had never had such a facility and does not particularly want to start using one now. In between her bath days she uses her basin to wash her face. When a care staff assistant arrives, they walk with her to the bathroom, help her undress and use the hoist in the specialist bath to place her into the water. Rose had always enjoyed taking baths and she still does, although with the pressures on staff time she cannot have a long soak in the water, which she liked when she was younger. She finds it demeaning having to be naked while a relative stranger helps her wash, but she says she remains stoical and tries not to think about it too much. Besides, the same care assistants have been helping her for the past few months, and they are friendly and help make the experience less embarrassing by sharing a joke. Nevertheless, when there are agency staff who are helping residents, Rose prefers not to have a bath if she can avoid it.[1]

10 a.m.–12 noon. Once Rose has finished her bath and has dressed again, she makes her way to the arts and crafts room, which is fairly busy today. Some of the residents are making pottery, while others are knitting, but Rose has been working on a watercolour for the past few weeks. She does not have any real friends in the home. She says she tries her best to be friendly, but at her age she feels it is too late to form proper friendships. Nevertheless, she feels that it is important to remain mentally active and not to lose one's faculties, although she is becoming frustrated by her failing eyesight. Her arm has also never really recovered well enough to be able to paint like she did when she was younger.

12 noon–1 p.m. Lunch is served from noon, and residents line themselves up beforehand. Residents have a menu with two possible options. Rose likes the food, although many others complain: some think the food is 'too modern', while others think that it is not up to 'hotel' standards.

1–2 p.m. After lunch, Rose makes her way to a physiotherapy class. Here a physiotherapist leads a group of ten residents through a series of exercises that are designed to maintain and strengthen their physical capabilities. Residents sit on chairs in a circle while the physiotherapist leads them through various exercises. Rose finds the stretching exercises fairly manageable, but she has much more difficulty when she is asked to stand up from the chair directly without using her arms for support.

2–6 p.m. After the class Rose returns to her floor. Sometimes during the afternoons her daughter comes to visit, but not today. There are continuing activities in the arts and crafts room, but Rose is feeling tired and does not have the patience. On her floor a number of residents are seated in the wing-backed chairs and are sleeping. Some of these residents spend almost their entire days seated there. Staff face a difficult balancing act between allowing 'clients' the choice and independence to do what they wish, and knowing that if they do not take part in activities they will very quickly deteriorate, both physically and mentally. Rose spends the afternoon in her bedroom listening to classical music on her radio. At 3 p.m. afternoon tea is served in the dining room, but Rose does not attend.

6–7 p.m. At dinnertime residents can also choose between two meals, but Rose is not very hungry. The care staff encourage her to eat more, but she mostly picks at the food.

7–11 p.m. After dinner there is a discussion group in one room, and a film playing in another. On her floor there is a residents' meeting to discuss the running of the home, but Rose decides to go to her room, read a book and listen to the radio. At 10 p.m. she decides to go to bed, and a care assistant comes to help her undress and put on her nightgown. Around 11 p.m., Rose falls asleep.

Case-study 2: 'Alfred'

Alfred lives in a specialized dementia unit attached to a small residential care home catering for forty people. The average age of residents is 92, and the majority have some form of cognitive functioning difficulty, although most are able to wash and dress themselves. The dementia unit caters for five residents and has its own lounge, bathroom and kitchen, separate from the rest of the home. Alfred's room consists of a hospital-style bed, an armchair and dressing table. Residents in most of the rooms in the home are decorated with photographs, pictures and ornaments, but Alfred's room is sterile-looking with no decorations except for three family photographs. There is an en-suite bathroom, consisting of a toilet, basin and shower (although this is never used because care staff would get soaked if they tried to wash residents in it).

Alfred was born in Leeds, but has lived in the care home for the past year. He suffers from Alzheimer's disease, so that his memory—particularly his short-term memory—is extremely limited. He has three sons, but his wife, who had previously cared for him, died last year.

7–8 a.m. Alfred has slept fitfully. He is doubly incontinent, and the night care staff needed to change his incontinence pads twice during the night. At 7.30 a.m. the night care worker wakes him, helps him out of his bed and washes his hands and face for breakfast.

8–10 a.m. At 8 o'clock, the day member of staff takes over from the night worker, and there is a brief 'hand-over' when they discuss the status of the residents and any issues that have arisen since the last shift. The day worker makes the residents their breakfast, which is served individually in their own rooms. Breakfast for Alfred consists of porridge, toast and orange juice. After breakfast, he is taken to the toilet. Three times a week residents in the unit are bathed, which most find fairly traumatic: according to a care staff member, 'if you heard the crying and screaming that takes place during bathing (especially when hair is being washed) you'd think I was killing them'. Today is not a bath day for Alfred, and the care staff member washes him down while he is still sitting on the toilet (a practice known as 'strip-washing'). After he has been washed, he is then dressed and moved into the lounge area where he sits on one of the high wing-backed chairs.

10 a.m.–12.30 p.m. There are no dedicated activities for residents this morning. While smaller homes may be able to promote a more 'family' environment than larger institutions, a key downside is a lack of resources and staff able to provide a wide range of activities throughout each day. Yesterday, an aromatherapist visited the unit, and she played relaxing music and massaged residents' feet using essential oils. Today, the care staff puts on some 'old-time' music for the residents, and they sit in their chairs until 11 o'clock, when they have their mid-morning cup of tea.

12.30–2 p.m. Lunch is served at 12.30, with the food being cooked by the central kitchen and brought over to the unit. Food in the home is cooked on a four-week rota, with residents given a choice at suppertime of what they would like to eat the next day. Today is a Friday, and residents are given the choice of a starter of chicken soup, fresh grapefruit or fruit juice, followed by a main course of hot or cold roast chicken or cold meat, with roast potatoes and seasonal vegetables, and a dessert of lemon meringue pie, ice cream or fresh fruit. After lunch, they are offered lemon tea or black coffee. Because it is a Jewish home, the mixing of 'meat' and 'dairy' dishes is forbidden; hence after the meal residents are not allowed a hot drink containing milk. Once he has finished his lunch, Alfred is once again toiletted and his incontinence pads are changed.

2–5 p.m. At 2 o'clock, residents in the unit are brought over to the home's main lounge where bingo is taking place. None of the dementia unit residents are able to take part in the activity, but they sit in their chairs and watch what goes on. At 3.30 afternoon tea is served. Alfred sometimes has visits from one of his sons or daughters-in-law, but this can be extremely traumatic for relatives. A recent letter to the *Jewish Chronicle*—British Jewry's largest circulation weekly newspaper—makes the point particularly eloquently and emotionally:

> I visit my 94 year-old mother in a Jewish home. Sometimes these visits are very enjoyable, and on occasions we can even have a laugh together, while at other times she is distressed, wanting to know 'why she is there' or 'was she so horrible a person that no one ever wanted to marry her' (my dad died three years ago, after them being married for 73 years), 'why her mum and dad never visit her' and so on. During the visits, she frequently asks who I am. She says that she knows I 'belong to her' but doesn't know how. In the hour-or-so that I am there, she asks 20 to 30 times if I am her son, and each time that I confirm that I am she looks at me in amazement, as though it were the first, and then cries for a few seconds. These are but a few of the traumas I go through during the visits ... The emotional strain of seeing what my mother is now, and recalling what she was a few years ago, is hard to bear. At times, I find myself unable to face the stress of visiting.[2]

5–8 p.m. At 5 o'clock care staff return Alfred and the other four residents to the special unit to get ready for dinner. At 6 o'clock all of the residents go to the main dining room for the Friday night Sabbath service. During the summer, a local rabbi usually leads the prayers and the blessings of the wine and bread, but during the winter it is much harder to find people willing to lead the service. When the days are shorter, it is difficult to find people who are willing to walk to the care home (Jewish law forbids driving on the Sabbath) and so one of the male residents leads the service. All the men cover their heads with a *yarmulke* (skullcap), and the traditional prayers are recited, followed by a glass of kosher *kiddush* wine. Those that want to wash their hands (according to religious ritual) will then do so, followed by the appropriate prayer. Next, the blessing for the bread is recited; it is then cut into small pieces, dipped in salt and passed to all the residents. The Friday night meal is then served. Many homes base this meal around the traditional food of chicken, but in this home the main course tonight is salmon (by having a fish meal, residents can have tea or coffee with milk afterwards, which is what most people here prefer). For starters there are portions of sweet chopped herring on a bed of lettuce, followed by vegetable soup with *lokschen* (vermicelli noodles); the main course is baked salmon, roast and boiled potatoes, and green beans, and dessert is trifle, with cheese and biscuits. After dinner, some care homes will recite grace, but in this home the care staff help residents to leave the table. A number of residents then congregate in the lounge for a while, but Alfred is returned to the special unit, where he is toiletted, washed and made ready for bed.

Case-study 3: 'Miriam'

Miriam has lived for the past four months in a medium-sized Jewish nursing home. She moved to the home after a lengthy stay in hospital, following a stroke. She has limited movement down her left side, and the stroke has also affected her speech. Her three children helped her choose the care home, primarily because it is close to where they live, it is Jewish and they had also heard that it has a good reputation. Miriam's room is small, with a hospital-style bed, a dresser and a washbasin. The bathroom is not en-suite and the floor is hard hospital 'lino', although the rooms are due for redevelopment. The home is divided into three floors, with around a dozen residents on each. Each floor has its own dining room, television lounge, toilets, bathrooms, storerooms and sluice.

Midnight–7.30 a.m. Miriam has not been sleeping well. She has an ulcer on her leg that is proving difficult to clear and is causing her pain. Throughout the night, the nursing and care staff have been in to see her. Most of the rooms have a sidelight left on all night so that staff need not wake the residents or shine a torch on them when they check on them. The doors of the rooms are designed to open and close without making a noise so as to avoid waking residents. Miriam suffers from incontinence, and staff have had to help her to the toilet across the corridor twice during the night. At 6 a.m., a nurse brings her a cup of tea and helps her to sit up.

7.30–9.15 a.m. At 7.30 the day staff take over from those on night duty and, after a ten-minute handover, they set out about visiting residents who are, by and large, already awake. Residents are given a 'top-and-tail' wash (i.e. their face is cleaned, incontinence pads are changed and they are wiped down), and are then helped out of bed. Ideally two people should be used to help residents out of bed, but because of a shortage in staff numbers only one nurse helps Miriam, which she does with the help of an electric hoist. The nurse helps her to get dressed and puts her in a wheelchair after which she takes her to breakfast, which starts at 8.30. Breakfast lasts for around forty minutes, and during this time the nursing sister comes round with the medications. Miriam has medication to keep her blood pressure in check and she is also on antidepressants and antibiotics to help her with a chest infection. Miriam has trouble eating her food, so a care assistant helps to feed her.

9.15–10.15 a.m. After breakfast, a care assistant returns her to her room, and runs a bath for her. Once this is ready, Miriam is helped across the corridor, and then to undress. She is then seated in the hoist, which is manually raised and moved over the bath, which then electronically rises up. Bathing is done quickly, because Miriam finds it hard to sit up independently and also because of pressures on staff time. Once she has been bathed, she is raised up and out, and dried down. Although it is very hot in the bathroom, Miriam gets cold very quickly; however, drying older people requires care because their skin breaks down very easily. Miriam is then dressed (for the second time today) and returned to her room, where one of the nurses puts a new dressing on her leg. Miriam likes most of the staff members, although there is an 'enforced jollity' that sometimes annoys her.

10.15 a.m.–1 p.m. The doctor was supposed to visit today to review her medication, but he had to cancel and so Miriam spends the morning in the lounge watching day-time television. At noon she is wheeled into the dining room to eat lunch, and at this time she also receives her second round of medications.

1–3 p.m. Miriam is wheeled round to the room where arts and crafts are taking place. Because of the limited use of her left side, there is not much that she feels able to do, and the activities organizer has her hands full with several other residents who are making pottery. Miriam spends much of her time watching other people take part in activities. Because of her limited communication abilities following the stroke she feels that people often ignore her and concentrate on those who seem more able to take part in activities.

3–6 p.m. Miriam is wheeled back to her room and then back to the lounge, where the television is still on. At 4 o'clock, one of the befriender volunteers who sometimes visit the home comes round. She stays with Miriam for three-quarters of an hour, and they talk about her life as a child in the East End of Glasgow. It is the highlight of her day.

6–7 p.m. Dinner is served at 6 o'clock, and medications are once again given out.

7–10 p.m. After dinner, Miriam returns to her room where she listens to her radio for a while. A resident three doors down is calling incessantly for a nurse, who arrives, but ten minutes later the calling begins again. Miriam spent part of the Second World War in a concentration camp, and she says that she uses the same techniques she learned then for switching off outside noises by those who are, in her words, 'mentally defective'. At 8 o'clock her son rings her on the phone in her bedroom and he tells her the latest news about the family. At 10 o'clock, a care assistant helps her to get into her nightgown and then into bed.

Institutional life

The care provided by Jewish communities within residential and nursing homes inevitably varies in terms of the size of institution, ethos, facilities available and levels of support. Nonetheless, the three case-studies reveal much about the daily characteristics of life in Jewish residential and nursing care homes, and the strengths and weaknesses of current institutional provision. In the first part of this section some of the strengths of current provision will be highlighted, including the standards of many facilities, the commitment of staff and volunteers, and sensitivity to religious and cultural concerns. In the second part some of the weaknesses of current provision will be discussed, including issues of institutionalization, the (passive) encouragement of dependency, lack of stimulation and rehabilitation, problems in developing an effective client-centred approach, limitations in staffing and volunteer levels, and questions of institutional ethos and the overall models for how care to older people is provided. In many ways Jewish voluntary sector care homes are the 'best of the best' in terms of the care and facilities they provide. As such, the problems they face have important implications not only for the UK Jewish community, but also for care homes across the country, many of which do not have the same levels of community and financial support.

Strengths in the provision of Jewish institutional care

In recent years Jewish organizations have invested millions of pounds in building new care homes and updating facilities. Replacing and refurbishing facilities is an ongoing process with much work still needing to be done before all thirty-six Jewish voluntary sector care homes fully meet the national minimum standards introduced by the government, particularly in terms of size of bedrooms (see Chapter 3). Nevertheless, the overall standard of these care homes has improved dramatically over the past twenty years, with the vast majority of residents having their own rooms (many of which are en-suite), new arts and crafts centres, redesigned eating areas and lounges, redeveloped gardens and new physiotherapy facilities (one care home, for example, has invested in a hydrotherapy pool). Some care homes have also started to introduce computing facilities, although these are still very much in their infancy (see Chapter 9). New developments undoubtedly make a major difference to the quality of people's lives, with modern facilities helping to limit some of the effects of institutionalization that have dogged care homes since Poor Law times. With no government financial support for these developments, they have almost entirely depended on the contributions of local communities and wealthy philanthropists. In addition, some care homes have built specialist facilities for residents suffering from dementia, including reminiscence and multi-sensory rooms, which help to ease levels of anxiety.

Bricks-and-mortar developments are important to people's quality of life, but arguably the primary factor is the individual care provided to residents by members of staff and volunteers.

> What matters most to people is the 'caring-ness' of the individual. If somebody's taking me to the toilet—which is absolutely dominating my life because I can't do it anymore—it's the way they do it, how gentle they are, how caring, how they respect my dignity. It's that individual relationship that a person forms, or doesn't form, that is the largest quality factor to somebody's life (care home employee).

Almost all residents and family members interviewed spoke very highly of the staff working in Jewish voluntary sector care homes: 'they were very, very good, very caring ... I'm sure that's because of the leadership, the person in charge.' This, of course, also relates to volunteers who play an important role in befriending residents, helping to run activities and contributing to the maintenance of a Jewish ethos. In many ways, volunteers are the 'added value' that allows Jewish residential and nursing homes to maintain their standards of care (see Chapter 8).

> The best thing about the home was the staff, the staff gave the atmosphere there. I think they were wonderful, right from the top down, they were all so

> pleasant, even down to those who swept the floors, they were very personal and nice—but I would have preferred more staff, particularly those who did the activities, and there's a need for more volunteers (relative of care home resident).

Interviewees were often acutely aware of limitations in the number of staff and volunteers, and of the fact that some are not well trained. Moreover, despite the caring attitudes of most staff, others expressed concern that they inadvertently help to institutionalize residents, and that they, and care homes in general, sometimes fail to appreciate people's individuality.

Jewish residential and nursing care homes also provide facilities and an environment sensitive to people's spiritual and religious needs. Mixing with people of similar religious, cultural or social backgrounds is clearly of huge importance to many residents and to their quality of life (see also Chapter 6). Indeed, religion and spirituality are known to be significant coping resources for people suffering (or for people whose close relatives and friends are suffering) from long-standing illnesses or disabilities.[3] Jewish voluntary sector care homes have a long tradition of providing kosher and Jewish-style food, as well as centring their activities around the Jewish calendar, the different festivals and the Sabbath. These care homes are—in principle at least—also able to deal sensitively with Jewish attitudes and rites relating to death and bereavement in ways that non-Jewish homes would find difficult.

Jewish voluntary sector care homes provide many services that are of the very highest quality and this is a point of pride for the UK Jewish community. Many of the families and the older people themselves interviewed for this study stated they were happy or very happy with the homes and the care provided. Nevertheless, while the successes of care homes and the improvements made over the past twenty years should be recognized, fundamental weaknesses in the system remain.

Weaknesses in the provision of Jewish institutional care

Policymakers and academics have studied institutions—large bricks-and-mortar constructions such as prisons, hospitals, asylums and 'homes for the aged'—for many years. Arguably the two most important figures in these debates have been the French historian and philosopher Michel Foucault, and the American sociologist Erving Goffman.[4] Both these authors were concerned with issues of power and control, and how the environments of institutions, and the regimes of staff, seek to 'restrain, control, treat, "design" and "produce" particular and supposedly improved versions of human minds and bodies'.[5] While also concerned with how individuals resist the system, both examined some of the fundamental problems relating to how society deals with those no longer able (or allowed) to live independently. They argued that the institutional worlds of these asylums and prisons 'dispossess', and then try to recreate the identities and roles of inmates through the routines of their everyday lives and the processes of institutionalization.[6]

Goffman's and Foucault's descriptions of institutions are often extremely dark and disturbing. Neither, however, directly investigated care homes for older people. The author most associated with these institutions is Peter Townsend, whose seminal work *The Last Refuge* (1962) is a scathing indictment of the lack of changes since Poor Law times. He argued that these institutions lead to isolation from family, friends and community, a collapse of self-determination and new relationships with other residents and staff that are markedly tenuous. In one of the most damning passages of his report, he describes his first visit to a former workhouse in 1957:

> The first impression was grim and sombre. A high wall surrounded some tall Victorian buildings, and the entrance lay under a forbidding arch with a porter's lodge at one side. The asphalt yards were broken up by a few beds of flowers but there was no garden worthy of the name. Several hundred residents were housed in large rooms on three floors. Dormitories were overcrowded, with ten or twenty iron-framed beds close together, no floor covering and little furniture other than ramshackle lockers. The day-rooms were bleak and uninviting. In one of them sat forty men in high-backed Windsor chairs, staring straight ahead or down at the floor. They seemed oblivious of what was going on around them. The sun was shining but no one was looking that way ... Life seemed to have been drained from them, all but the dregs.[7]

Townsend wanted to know why so many people still lived in residential homes given that many could remain in the community. In a later article he argued that residential care home living leads to 'structured dependency', whereby older people are presumed to be more dependent than they actually are or need to be.[8] Society associates old age with negative characteristics—infirmity, loss of intellectual ability, dementia, dependency, lack of worth—and this determines expectations as well as the policies determining how 'they' are catered for. This ties into more recent academic and policy debates about the 'social construction' of old age and the problems of ageism.[9] Indeed a great deal of research in recent years has highlighted major problems of discrimination within the health and social care sectors as well as the abuse of older people within institutional settings.[10]

There is no doubt that care homes have come a long way since authors such as Townsend published their condemnations, with improvements being driven in part by changing attitudes to older people, a greater involvement of families, as well as the more direct influences of government legislation. Indeed, the structured dependency thesis has been the focus of several recent critiques. In particular, it has been criticized for failing to recognize the poverty of many people's lives before they moved to care homes and the fact that many residents welcome the opportunity not to have to struggle on their own any more. Moreover, criticisms of care homes may reflect wider societal prejudices against group living.[11] These points certainly need to be recognized, but by the same measure it is also clear that problems of institutionalized living remain, even within the most modern care homes. In the case-studies, the queuing up of residents before breakfast, the ways in which they passively wait while meals are served to them, and the (resident) insistence of meal-time dress-codes highlight how residential and nursing care can very quickly 'fix' people within particular routines and regimes so that they lose their independence.

One of the main strategies discussed in the academic and policy literature to help overcome the negative associations of institutionalized living—and indeed of services for older people more generally—is *user empowerment*.[12] There has been a growing recognition (in theory if not always in practice) that older people should be cared for not out of a paternalistic duty—services provided *to* the needy—but rather as individuals who should be as involved as possible in the decisions and activities that affect *their* lives.

> [User empowerment] refers to a change in power relationships whereby the focus of services is to assist the individual to achieve his or her goals. Enabling a person to achieve independence has implications for the type of support provided, as well as for the manner in which it is delivered. Many service users' experiences of services are quite different from such a model, and accounts of patronising and oppressive services that do not deliver what is wanted are frequently encountered. A lack of choice over how and when services are delivered, and having to fit in with service routines, rather than having services that respond to individual needs, are illustrative of [this] lack of power.[13]

Groups such as Age Concern and Help the Aged have advocated ideas of partnership and openness, so that decisions are made according to the needs and wants of older people, i.e. a 'bottom-up' approach. This is radically different from the 'top-down' approach of most traditional types of institution, where the lives of 'inmates' are carefully controlled and ordered by senior management, and the rules, regulations and lifestyles are enforced or created by frontline staff. Despite the advances of recent years, many care homes still view people as *passive recipients* of care, rather than fully accepting models that call for residents and their families to be *active stakeholders*.

Researchers have highlighted the problems of dependency for many years, in, for example, the psychological studies undertaken by Ellen Langer in the United States. In one 'classic' study Langer and her colleagues divided residents in a nursing home into two groups. The first group was emphatically encouraged to make more decisions for themselves, for example, by choosing where to receive visitors or what films to show in the home and when. They were also given a houseplant and had to make decisions about how to care for it, such as when and how much water to provide and whether to put it in the window or to shield it from too much sun. The second group was not encouraged to make decisions for themselves, but were told that staff were there to help them in every way possible. Eighteen months later, the first group had greater levels of physical activity, were more sociable and had higher health evaluation levels than the second group. Moreover, mortality rates for the first group were fifty per cent lower than in the second.[14]

> Surprisingly, we found a lot of unintentional resistance—from families and the elderly themselves—to our attempts to give them more control and make them more independent. As in many institutional settings, dependency is unwittingly but flagrantly encouraged. When a nursing home resident is helped to dress for breakfast (either out of concern for the resident or to save time for the staff), he or she may feel incompetent and helpless. Ultimately such help will take more of the staff's time, since the more help people are given, the more help they will come to need ... When the will to act is thwarted, it atrophies into a wish to be taken care of.[15]

In Jewish homes similar processes of dependency occur, as illustrated by the three case-studies. For example, bathing typically takes place according to the routines of the care home, meals are provided at set times, and activities are often determined and arranged by co-ordinators rather than by older people themselves. The case-studies also show how, in each twenty-four-hour period, residents may actually do remarkably little.

One senior care worker explained how limitations in staffing levels (see also Chapter 8) mean that staff members are having to work extremely hard to complete the essential tasks of providing residents with nursing and personal care. As such, there is very little time for rehabilitation, beyond that supplied by any physiotherapists who may be based in, or who regularly visit, the home. This interviewee argued that, for example, someone recovering from a stroke should be encouraged to learn to feed themselves, but because of a lack of time—and appropriate training and mentorship—staff too often do the task for them. Similarly, it is all too easy to put a person in a wheelchair to take them to an activity or to the toilet—as in Miriam's case—rather than using the move from one place to another as an opportunity to help them walk and regain their powers of mobility. This interviewee argued that the 'structure is set up to suit the staff, we just don't think in client-centred ways'.

One nurse with experience of several Jewish residential and nursing homes argued that there is a failure to view the needs of each client in an individual or *holistic* manner. One professional spoke of residents being 'bored out of their eyeballs' and complained that far too much time was spent watching 'that damned television'. This person believed that, contra the stated ethos of the home, residents often view it as 'God's waiting room ... they come here to die'. Moreover, the lack of stimulation and, of crucial importance, the lack of motivation mean that many 'get dementia while they are here'. Another interviewee argued that there is a 'culture of passivity', so that as long as residents are not causing difficulties they will not be encouraged to do more:

> The home is very good at looking after the physical side of people's care, but not as good at the social, mental

side. It's good for people who are active, but not for those who are more passive ... It's fine giving them nice food, but no one does anything for their minds (relative of a care home resident).

Such problems can be especially severe in smaller care homes—as Alfred's case-study clearly shows—in which there are not the resources to fund full-time activity organizers. Furthermore, even when activities are organized they tend to focus on those who are actively able to take part. Accordingly, while events such as arts and crafts or a game of bingo may be arranged, a large number may not be able, or indeed be willing, to take part and thus they may go for days without being involved in activities. An interviewee in a small Jewish home admitted that, because of a lack of time with residents, 'a number of residents have actually lost the power of speech'. Another social service professional argued that 'there are some Jewish organizations that just touch the surface of quality of life'. These disturbing admissions suggest a need for a rethink by managers, staff and community. Instead of looking from an institutional perspective at the range of services provided, there is a need to look at each client and review what they, *as individuals*, are doing and what they require.

Beyond major questions about resources and levels of staffing (discussed in Chapter 8), a key source of these problems is arguably the overall models of care adopted by residential and nursing homes. According to the national minimum standards imposed by the government, all homes must have care plans for each resident. Such care plans highlight the needs of residents and the care that should be provided. However, it should be noted that there are several different models for care plans that can radically affect how care is delivered and, more importantly, the ethos and expectations of residents and staff. Care homes (and hospitals) commonly base their care plans on the classic nursing model, devised by Nancy Roper, Winifred Logan and Alison Tierney, that lists twelve 'activities of living' that should be maintained, such as breathing, eating and drinking, communicating, expressing sexuality, sleeping and dying.[16] Care plans based on this model will take the form of sheets of paper that list the nature of particular problems, the needs of care clients, and an evaluation of the outcome of care. Such models—which actually trace their roots back to Henry Ford's attempts to improve production at his car plants—tend to be rather mechanistic. Nevertheless, other care models are available (such as those designed by Imogene King, Dorothea Orem or Callista Roy) that take more holistic approaches to care, emphasizing the goal of increasing independence and self-determination.[17] These latter models are often adopted by hospices, and indeed there is much that can be learned from other forms of care and the different types of ethos they adopt. The start of this process must be research into the possibilities and effectiveness of different models of care and a real consideration and debate of the purpose of care homes in the Jewish community, and their aspirations for each individual resident.

Connected with strategies for promoting user involvement are schemes that actively consult and survey residents and their families about service provision.[18] Such strategies are well developed in some Jewish voluntary sector organizations and sectors of the care industry, but almost non-existent in others. For example, Jewish housing associations are required as registered social landlords to produce regular tenant satisfaction surveys to ensure that standards are maintained. Until the recent Care Standards Act, however, there have been no overall UK requirements for care homes to run customer satisfaction surveys or to involve residents and families in decision-making in other ways. Nevertheless, some Jewish homes and organizations have already developed strategies for improving user involvement. For example, in Miriam's case-study, there is an organized residents' forum. However, several interviewees identified problems inherent in such schemes and pointed out a clear gap between the ideals advocated in the policy and academic literature, and the day-to-day realities of trying to involve residents and their families.

> An issue which has now been raised by the licensing authority is what we're doing with regard to customer satisfaction surveys. We're about to do a customer satisfaction survey for relatives, that's easy, but it's more difficult to do with residents. Many of the people are physically not able to complete the questionnaires, either for physical reasons, they're just too frail, or they've got dementia and can't do it. The answer might be to devise a simple questionnaire, and then get volunteers to go round and talk to people (care home manager).

In addition to formal customer satisfaction surveys, which can tend to package people's views within pre-existing categories and ideas, some care homes also have regular residents' forums. These forums allow individuals to raise concerns, and discuss areas in which improvements can be made.[19] Nevertheless, other providers believed that such meetings were impossible given the reality of the nature of their residents.

> It's very difficult to conduct meaningful interviews with residents, they want to talk about the past, they really

don't want to talk about the home. There are often four or five mentally alert people, and what they hate most is being in a home with people who are demented. From talking to people in homes, they're not happy, but you can't say they're not happy because the care isn't good enough, they're not happy because they're 95, they've been independent all their lives, they can't do anything anymore, they can't read, they can't walk anymore, they've lost everyone who is dear to them. It's very difficult to separate out the quality of care they receive, from their absolute hatred of the fact that they're there (social service professional).

Other providers spoke about some residents' meetings in the past at which the comments were so personal as to be useless ('she didn't iron my shirt properly' or 'I lost my cardigan'), although useful comments did come from other more active residents. Another manager did not arrange such forums because of a few 'dominators' who he believed would prevent others from expressing their views. This manager preferred to approach individuals on a regular one-to-one basis to determine the strengths and weaknesses of the home. In other homes, independent advocates are used, who are trained to speak on behalf of vulnerable people unable to speak for themselves. Since different homes clearly have different client constituencies and levels of activity and frailty, methods of involving residents will necessarily vary across the sector.

In addition to accessing the views of residents themselves, providers are also often encouraged to incorporate and involve the families of older people in the running of homes. Again, this is common practice in some homes, although others considered such schemes unnecessary.

> We've never done customer satisfaction surveys, but we're very certain that Jewish people in general, Jewish children [in particular] very much let us know if we're delivering good care. They're very demanding, but some are very grateful ... We're acutely aware of our shortcomings and areas we need to strengthen up by people who are not backwards about coming forward (care home manager).

The sense of families of residents being over-demanding was a common feature of a number of interviews. Nevertheless, without a suitable space for families to express their concerns and fears, a confrontational attitude towards social care provision may be difficult to avoid. Several interviewees with relatives in care homes argued that they would have liked more consultation and involvement, although others were 'not really bothered'. Indeed, one professional who had instituted a monthly relatives' meeting found a lot of apathy: 'people don't have the time. I'm all for it, everybody will be for it, but to organize it is a different matter.' Still, if service providers are to recognize fully the implications of user involvement and empowerment—and indeed meet their registration requirements—strategies for furthering the involvement of clients in the running of their home will need to be devised. Interviewees with family members resident in care homes sometimes, though certainly not always, expressed feelings of isolation and detachment from care homes, and this a problem that needs to be addressed.

Ideas of user empowerment are in part supported, but also in many ways contradicted, by the approach that many care homes have chosen to adopt, which is to style themselves as 'hotels with care'. Such an approach has the advantage of stressing the importance of residents who are specifically thought of as 'clients', with the power to choose between different organizations. In theory, this should help develop higher service standards, as facilities explicitly focus their aims on meeting client expectations.[20] Nevertheless, the actual ability of older people to make consumerist choices between different care options is, as Chapter 6 discussed, often more myth than reality. Moreover, a re-branding of a care home as a hotel-type facility may be more cosmetic than actual, being primarily designed to 'sell' the quality of services to prospective relatives of older people, and to ease the pain and guilt associated with moving a loved one into a residential or nursing home. While this may indeed help to soften the blow of a person having to move from their own home, it can also have the (unintended) effect of establishing from the outset a 'top-down' approach to care in which older people very quickly become dependent on nursing and care staff. A person living in their own home has a number of responsibilities in terms of making personal decisions, ranging from what food to cook, when to get up or who to let in the door (whether friends, relatives or social service professionals). In hotels many of these decisions are taken away, as staff look after guests who are encouraged to do as little as possible for themselves and to be pampered. Staying in hotels can be very enjoyable for a few weeks; over time, however, they begin to lose their appeal. Introducing a culture of dependency within care homes necessarily has extremely negative long-term connotations for residents' health and happiness.

Conclusions

Jewish residential and nursing homes in the United Kingdom have a long and distinguished history, providing care to thousands of Jews in environments designed to be sensitive to their social, cultural and religious needs. Many of these care homes are of the very highest quality, providing outstanding levels of service. At the same time, however, there are concerns and challenges facing the sector, particularly in terms of countering processes of institutionalization and dependency. Many care homes try to include imaginative activities and events for residents to keep their bodies and minds active. However, the stereotypical image of residents sitting in high wing-backed chairs around the edge of lounges, saying nothing to each other, is all too real. Even in the best homes in the country clear processes of institutionalization remain, despite the considerable efforts of management and staff.

Care homes are often simplistically presented as either all good or all bad. The reality is, however, far more complex. Care homes can provide support, friendship, fun and care in ways that may be impossible for those living in their own homes, who may suffer from isolation, depression and an inability to look after themselves. At the same time, though, care homes are sometimes feared as places of isolation, boredom, loss of independence and the final stage before death. There is a need for an honest debate about current forms of care home provision, as well as broader questions about whether these really are the best way to look after older people with physical or mental frailties, or whether there are other models that can be adopted (see Chapter 9). However, before any changes can be considered, an understanding of the key strategic issues facing providers—and hence the barriers to improvements—need to be recognized, and these are examined in the following chapter.

Notes

1. For an excellent discussion of the issues involved in the bathing of older people and the implications of people losing the ability to bathe themselves, see Julia Twigg, *Bathing—The Body and Community Care* (London: Routledge 2000).
2. Letter to the editor by Paul Klein, 'Painful side of visiting the aged', *Jewish Chronicle*, 21 September 2001.
3. Jon Stuckey, 'Blessed assurance: the role of religion and spirituality in Alzheimer's disease caregiving and other significant life events', *Journal of Ageing Studies*, vol. 15, 2001, 69–84. See also David Gracie and John Vincent, 'Progress report: religion and old age', *Ageing and Society*, vol. 18, 1998, 101–10.
4. Michel Foucault, *Madness and Civilisation* (London: Routledge 1967); Michel Foucault, *Discipline and Punish: The Birth of the Prison* (London: Penguin 1977); Erving Goffman, *Asylums: Essays on the Social Situation of Mental Patients and Other Inmates* (London: Penguin 1961).
5. Chris Philo and Hester Parr, 'Institutional geographies: introductory remarks', *Geoforum*, vol. 31, 2000, 513–21 (513).
6. See also Peace, Kellaher and Willcocks.
7. Townsend, 4.
8. Peter Townsend, 'The structured dependency of the elderly: the creation of social policy in the twentieth century', *Ageing and Society*, vol. 1, 1981, 5–28.
9. See Chris Phillipson and Neil Thompson, 'The social construction of old age: new perspectives on the theory and practice of social work with older people', in Rosemary Bland (ed.), *Developing Services for Older People and Their Families* (London and Bristol, PA: Jessica Kingsley 1996), 13–25.
10. See Home Office/Department of Health, *No Secrets: Guidance on Developing and Implementing Multi-agency Policies and Procedures to Protect Vulnerable Adults from Abuse* (London:

Home Office 2000); Jacki Pritchard, *Male Victims of Elder Abuse: Their Experiences and Needs* (London: Jessica Kingsley 2001); Emilie Roberts, Janice Robinson and Linda Seymour, *Old Habits Die Hard: Tackling Age Discrimination in Health and Social Care* (London: King's Fund 2002).

11 Christine Oldman and Deborah Quilgars, 'The last resort? Revisiting ideas about older people's living arrangements', *Ageing and Society*, vol. 19, 1999, 363–84.

12 See, for example, Roger Blunden, *Terms of Engagement: Engaging Older People in the Development of Community Services* (London: King's Fund 1998); Department of Health, *National Service Framework*; Henwood.

13 Henwood, 62.

14 Ellen Langer, *Mindfulness: Choice and Control in Everyday Life* (London: Harvill 1989).

15 Ibid., 95–6.

16 Nancy Roper, Winifred Logan and Alison Tierney, *The Elements of Nursing* (Edinburgh: Churchill Livingstone 1990).

17 Imogene King, *A Theory for Nursing: System, Concept, Process* (New York: Wiley 1981); Dorothea Orem, *Nursing Concepts for Practice* (New York: McGraw 1980); Callista Roy, *Introduction to Nursing: An Adaptation Model* (London: Prentice-Hall 1984).

18 Linda Bauld, John Chesterman and Ken Judge, 'Measuring satisfaction with social care amongst older service users: issues from the literature', *Health and Social Care*, vol. 8, 2000, 316–24.

19 See Norma Raynes, 'Involving residents in quality specification', *Ageing and Society*, vol. 18, 1998, 65–78. See also Rocío Fernàndez-Ballesteros, Maria Zamarron and Miguel Angel Ruíz, 'The contribution of socio-demographic and psychosocial factors to life satisfaction', *Ageing and Society*, vol. 21, 2001, 25–43.

20 Rosemary Bland, 'Independence, privacy and risk: two contrasting approaches to residential care for older people', *Ageing and Society*, vol. 19, 1999, 539–60.

8 Institutional care: key strategic issues

The previous chapter discussed the characteristics of life in Jewish residential and nursing care homes and the strengths and weaknesses of current provision. While Jewish homes undoubtedly have many strengths, they also face a number of problems and challenges, particularly in relation to limiting the effects of processes of institutionalization. Identifying and acknowledging these difficulties is a key element in the process of modernization and reform, but improvements are also dependent on a range of other factors. The Jewish voluntary sector is not, as Chapters 2–4 showed, immune to wider societal influences, whether central government legislation, the policies and financial health of local authorities, national problems in staff recruitment, or the changing needs and expectations of care of the UK population. Over the last twenty years, the ideology of successive governments has been to adopt a market-orientated approach to care, with the result that voluntary sector services—especially those with formal government contracts—have had to meet ever higher standards of quality, while suffering from often severe funding limitations. For the Jewish voluntary sector, there is a difficult balancing act between funding and structural limitations (such as national staff shortages), and the desire to provide high-quality services to Jewish people in keeping with a Jewish ethos (however defined or understood). There is inevitably a trade-off between the needs and wants of clients, and the realities of organizational survival and development. This chapter examines this often uneasy relationship through a discussion of some of the key strategic issues facing Jewish residential and nursing care homes. The first part of the chapter examines the key challenge of *financing services*, especially given the enormous costs involved in running care home institutions and serious limitations in local authority funding. The second discusses the problem of estimating the likely *provision of places* needed in the future, which, especially given overall levels of population decline in the UK Jewish community, is of major concern. The final part examines issues relating to *human resources*, the difficulties faced by Jewish organizations in recruiting and retaining staff, and the associated problems of maintaining a Jewish ethos. These issues are examined in relation to institutional care homes, although many of them also resonate across the Jewish social care sector and are discussed in Chapter 9.

Financing services

Arguably the most pressing strategic issue for Jewish residential and nursing care homes relates to the financial resources available to them. While providing excellent care services certainly requires far more than money, it is also a truism that lack of financial resources limits the quality and quantity of services provided and the opportunities for future development. Nevertheless, institutional care is a multi-billion pound industry in the United Kingdom, and in the Jewish voluntary sector amounts to tens of millions of pounds. The size of the financing involved is evident when examining the average weekly costs involved in providing institutional care for individual clients. Jewish voluntary sector care homes contain a mixture of both private (fee-paying) clients and those who are funded by local authorities. As Table 8.1

shows, fees for private clients in Jewish voluntary homes can be extremely high—up to £850 per week—especially in London where costs (especially staffing costs) are often much higher than in the regions.

Table 8.1 **Average weekly fees for private clients in Jewish voluntary sector care homes, 2000**

	Residential home fees per week (£)	*Nursing home fees per week (£)*
London and South-east (mean) average	495	626
Regions (mean) average	351	426
Range	220–565	371–850
Overall (mean) average	445	533

Average fees for private clients in Jewish residential and nursing homes are considerably higher than the United Kingdom as a whole. In 1998 average fees for private clients nation-wide were estimated by the Royal Commission as being £275 per week for residential care and £350 per week in nursing homes.[1] This compares with £445 and £533 respectively in Jewish voluntary sector homes. Several factors might explain these differences. First, the majority of Jewish voluntary sector homes are in London, with inevitably higher costs for the purchase of land and the payment of staff. However, an analysis of fee-paying clients in private care homes in the London borough of Barnet—the borough with the highest number of Jews (see Chapter 4)—shows that costs for residential care are actually cheaper than in Jewish voluntary sector homes located in the capital, although nursing care is slightly more expensive (see Table 8.2).

Table 8.2 **Average weekly fees for private clients in UK care homes (1998) and in private homes in the London borough of Barnet (2001)**[2]

	Residential home fees per week (£)	Nursing home fees per week (£)
United Kingdom (all homes)	275	350
Barnet (private care homes)	434	642

A second possible factor in explaining the difference in price is that the figures for England and Wales relate to 1998, whereas those for Jewish homes are for 2000 (and in Barnet for 2001). Third, there are extra costs involved in providing kosher food and culturally appropriate facilities. Fourth, fees from private clients in some Jewish homes are used to subsidize the shortfall in funding from local authority clients (see later). Fifth, Jewish voluntary sector care homes may be taking in clients who are older and frailer and thus require more expensive levels of support. Sixth, Jewish homes may be providing services that are of a higher standard than those of the national average, and the maintenance of the type of facilities acceptable to many Jews is necessarily expensive. Finally, Jewish voluntary sector care homes may not be particularly efficient, raising questions as to whether or not they deliver best value for money.

While fees for private clients are often very high, most (although not all) Jewish voluntary sector homes have a majority of state-funded clients. With pressures on local authorities to reduce their spending, this is creating severe financial problems for individual institutional care providers. In particular, interviewees expressed concerns about the gap between local government funding available for providing care services and actual costs.

> Local authorities have put a ceiling on the amount of money per person they are willing to pay—the figures vary from borough to borough—sometimes it only comes to 75 per cent or 80 per cent of actual costs of care [and, in fact, can be much lower than this], so the charity has to make up the shortfall. It's been a long-time now since they gave 100 per cent of the costs (social service professional).

Several interviewees expressed concern that the gap between local authority funding and actual care costs is only going to widen, and that the Jewish community will—if it wants to maintain and increase standards of care—have to increase its financial contributions.

> Relative funding from local authorities is probably going to decline, so if the community wants those add-on extras, they'll have to pay for it. Now you can argue until the cows come home that this is wrong—the community care legislation says that members of ethnic minorities are entitled to culturally sensitive provision—but the truth of the matter is that if you want quality, you've got to pay for it (care home manager).

Care homes are at the mercy of the funding procedures of different local authorities, with individual older people's addresses determining the amount of money available for care, and even whether they are entitled to institutional provision in the first place. This is care by postcode. For example, one social worker complained of the great difficulties in persuading a particular local authority to accept that individual clients were meeting the criteria for residential or nursing home care: 'There is a constant pressure to save money, the criteria for obtaining long-term care are definitely getting harder [to meet].' This particular local authority had apparently overspent its budget, and so demanded a 50 per cent reduction in the numbers obtaining residential care, regardless of actual need. Another care home manager spoke of how a different local authority 'was particularly bad, ten people had to die before one could be admitted'. He spoke of a 'game of brinkmanship' with the local authorities. As a charity, they are obliged to take in Jewish people in need, but it is 'financial suicide' continually to take in those for whom the local council will not pay; if Jewish charities do this, they are effectively subsidizing the state. As such, it is often a case of 'who will crack first', the local authority's requirements to fund those needing long-term care, or the moral obligations of the Jewish organization. According to one social service provider, 'elderly people get such a raw deal, if they were children then people would be screaming'.

The new economic and political realities of welfare provision are clearly biting hard. One manager acknowledged that the home had suffered a loss of £300,000 the previous year, and that if this continued over any length of time then the charity could no longer remain solvent. Another admitted that 'we run at a loss, we're spending our capital reserves to offset our losses'. Other organizations spoke of resources being stretched to the limit trying to bridge the gap between local authority funding and the actual costs of care: 'there's an automatic expectation that the Jewish community will do what actually the government isn't doing and to do that without the resources.' Heathlands—Manchester's largest Jewish voluntary sector care home—recently reported an operational loss of £1.25 million.[3] At its annual meeting, the President, Joy Cainer, spoke of the enormous difficulties of obtaining local authority funding:

> It is difficult for us to obtain residents who meet the funding requirements. By the time funding is available, the patients have often deteriorated. For the first time in our existence we have a core vacancy of 25–30 empty beds ... Reluctantly we have downsized by 32 beds. Half of the first floor of Eventhall House is completely closed. This is very sad. 65 per cent of our residents are state funded. We have had to approach the families to help with our shortfall.[4]

Throughout the whole of the UK care sector it is estimated that almost 10,000 places in care homes for older and disabled people were lost in the year 2000, including some 760 individual (mostly nursing) homes. The independent sector (private and voluntary homes) lost a net 7,600 places, amounting to 1.6 per cent of total capacity. Closures were, unsurprisingly, most severe in the south of England.[5] According to one Jewish service provider, 'the crisis is already here ... this just can't go on'.

Shortages in central and local government funding necessarily put a greater burden on the Jewish community to fund services: 'what the government doesn't pay, the community must pay' (care home manager). Most capital funding comes (and always has come) from community sources, but the shortfalls in local authority revenue are putting increasing pressures on social care organizations. This, of course, applies to the spectrum of social services for older people, including domiciliary care and community day centres. Community centres, in fact, often receive relatively little state support despite the high costs involved and the large numbers of individuals who make use of them. Moreover, some councils provide 'cost ceilings' on the amounts they are willing to pay for services provided in people's homes, thus forcing people to move to institutional care prematurely. People receiving home care are expected to make a small contribution to the services they receive. Once they move to institutional care, they typically pay a much larger contribution towards costs, including monies from their state and occupational pensions, any income support they receive or monies from the sale of any assets they hold (see Chapter 3 for details). Accordingly, when the costs to councils of home care are greater than the amounts payable for institutional care (i.e. the amount a council is willing to pay institutional care providers, *minus* individuals' own contributions), people are forced to leave their homes. It is arguably illegal for councils to do this (although it has never been tested in a court of law), but the practice nevertheless goes on.

With a seemingly increased requirement for the Jewish community to fund social care services, several interviewees raised concern over the difficulties of raising money for service provision, human resource initiatives and core costs, rather than for bricks-and-mortar buildings. One interviewee described this as the 'edifice complex': 'people want to give money for something they can see.' Another social service provider argued that 'we've got so much work to educate our donors ... in our business it is the people that are the key issues'. This is not to say that bricks-and-mortar constructions are unimportant, or that the social environment is not a key component of people's quality of life. Nevertheless, other, 'more unseen' elements, such as high-quality staff training schemes are also of crucial importance and require financial support from the community.

Provision of places

A second key strategic issue for Jewish institutional providers relates to the future provision of places. The changes seen in the provision of formal care to older people across the United Kingdom discussed in Chapters 2 and 3 are set to continue, with major implications for the future provision of places by Jewish organizations. The increasing age and frailty of residents, together with the implications of demographic changes—particularly the growing proportion of Jews with non-Jewish spouses—poses serious and challenging questions for the Jewish voluntary sector. This is particularly so for sheltered housing organizations and care homes, where long-term investment in bricks and mortar is required. If organizations construct facilities that are in the wrong place or that are different from what the public wants and requires, the financial and social costs of these mistakes are high. Questions of geography are thus all-important.

> We are a small community, a diminishing community, how many old people are there in the community, how many will end up or need to go into homes, and of those that do need to go into homes, how many of them necessarily want to go into Jewish homes? (care home manager).

Across the United Kingdom, Jewish voluntary organizations have constructed new care homes and new facilities for older people, while also closing down older institutions. For example, the Heathlands home in Manchester is in the process of constructing new facilities for people with Alzheimer's disease, Jewish Care has recently opened a new residential home in Barnet (next to the large Lady Sarah Cohen home), and the old Newark Lodge home in Glasgow is being replaced by two brand-new homes. These developments are multi-million pound schemes, and reflect a desire by organizations to provide facilities of the very highest quality. They also reflect the need to replace facilities that are outdated, located in the wrong areas and would fail to meet incoming government legislation or the standards demanded by potential residents and their families. These new developments also reflect the changing needs of those in institutional care, as reflected in the increasing age of residents and, thus, the numbers categorized as elderly mentally infirm (EMI). Estimating future demand requires an understanding of these changes together with a nuanced understanding of likely future demands for care.

At present, some homes are over-subscribed with clients, while others are struggling to fill their places. According to one provider, all homes and organizations increasingly have to market themselves. Several providers spoke of having to adapt the ethos of their home to the model of a 'hotel with care' (although see Chapter 7 for some of the possible, unintended consequences of this), with the very latest facilities, adaptations and provisions for leisure.

> The sort of mentality many years ago was that these people—it was a very patronizing mentality—these people should be thankful that they're here, we're doing them the favour. That's all gone. We're not talking now about a bunch of old people, we're talking about clients, customers and they demand the best, and if they think that they won't get that here, they'll go somewhere else (care home manager).

In certain regional communities, Jewish residential and nursing homes have begun taking in non-Jews for the first time, reflecting the decline in the size of the Jewish population. This has implications for the ethos of these homes as specifically Jewish places, with one provider acknowledging that they would seriously consider downsizing if the number of non-Jews increased beyond 10 per cent: 'It's so special this home, it's very much part of the community, it's a major part of the community—if you're 50 per cent non-Jewish, it would not be a Jewish home.' These issues clearly affect declining regional communities but, even in Manchester and London, there are questions as to whether homes should take in non-Jewish spouses: 'we're going to have to consider the issue of the mixed-marriage generations' (care home manager). This manager spoke of how registration of the home by the Charity Commission was such that it is only allowed to take in members of the Jewish faith, although the home does not request evidence of Jewish status and takes people on trust.

> If we had an application from a mixed-married couple where the husband's Jewish and the wife is not Jewish, we couldn't take the wife, and that is a serious problem. It happens fairly rarely, but it will happen more in the future (care home manager).

The increase in the number of mixed marriages is a major complicating factor in planning future provision. Together with forecasting the impact of government legislation, the effects of demographic changes, the impact of the private sector and the likely future needs and wants of the populace, predicting future demand is extremely difficult and highly area-specific.

Human resources

Alongside issues of financing services and provision of places, the third key area for strategic planning purposes is human resources. Providing services to older people in an institutional care setting requires not only bricks-and-mortar buildings, but a whole range of other ingredients, most particularly the appropriate quantity and quality of paid and unpaid (volunteer) staff. These issues are set within the wider framework of the ongoing sea change in the delivery of services in the voluntary sector, from paternalistic approaches to professionalism:

> You've got to understand that the voluntary sector has been dragged into the twenty-first century. We started off eight years ago when I came in, we were a little charity that had some social work staff, one or two qualified staff, and the rest were unqualified volunteers. It was predominately a grant-giving welfare organization. It has been catapulted over the last few years (social service professional).

The increasing professionalization of organizations has major implications for the sector, and for the front-line staff and volunteers who deliver care. Some organizations are at the cutting edge of this process of professionalization, whilst others—typically those in smaller Jewish communities—still very much adopt a paternalistic attitude to care. With increasing professionalism usually come higher standards of care and models of good practice, but also an increase in bureaucracy and administration arguably at the expense of more 'tender' and more 'human' forms of care. These practical and attitudinal changes underpin the key human resource issues identified by service providers and other social service professionals, with three particular areas of concern emerging: recruitment and retention of general staff, Jewish recruitment and Judaism training, and volunteering.

Recruitment and retention of general staff

Caring for older people in formal institutional settings is a highly labour-intensive industry. There are 2,600 people employed in Jewish voluntary sector residential and nursing homes across Britain, 1,465 in London and the South-east, and 1,135 in the regions.[6] There is thus an approximate ratio of one member of staff (including administrative staff and management) for every resident, although not all who work in the sector do so on a full-time basis.

With a national shortage of care workers—particularly trained nursing staff—many Jewish voluntary sector homes face recruitment and retention difficulties. Several home owners spoke of the difficulties of obtaining registered nurses (RGNs), and hence an over-reliance in nursing and dual registered homes of care workers who may have little or no previous training or formal qualifications. The King's Fund inquiry into social care, *Future Imperfect?*, showed how almost three-quarters of care home staff have no qualifications, and argued that there is a correlation between poor training and poor workplace practice. Moreover, it is difficult to recruit staff in the first place given the often relatively low wages offered in the social care industry:

> With extended periods of staff shortages it is difficult to
> maintain the quality of support; hard to offer much one
> to one quality time with individuals and hard to
> maintain staff morale. With some supermarkets offering
> £8 per hour to stack shelves overnight it is hard to

> attract staff to a complex and often stressful job for
> much less money. In some parts of the country
> providers say that the only people applying for
> vacancies are those that McDonalds and Tesco have
> already rejected, and if employed they come with high
> numeracy and literacy training needs, quite apart from
> any induction training and values based training needs.[7]

Similarly, one manager of a Jewish voluntary sector care home argued that relatively low wages helped contribute to motivational problems.

> A lot of staff are not that well paid, and I think that if
> sometimes someone's not that well paid, and they find
> themselves in a job not by design but by need, it can be
> an uphill task to encourage them. I try to instil into the
> care staff that when we take a mother in, we're also
> taking in the family (care home manager).

Other managers and home-owners reported fewer recruitment and motivational problems: 'Our staff are very loyal. They treat the residents like family ... we're so lucky we have staff that stay, it makes a big difference.' Nevertheless, all those interviewed were extremely conscious of the importance of quality staff, and of maintaining a continuity of care.

Jewish recruitment and Judaism training

General staff recruitment problems are common across the social and health care sectors. However, for the Jewish community, there are further challenges and concerns relating to the recruitment of Jewish staff, and providing training in Jewish cultural and religious values and traditions. Only 4 per cent of staff working in Jewish voluntary sector care homes are Jewish. This figure includes management and administrative staff, as well as those working in the two homes that explicitly cater for strictly Orthodox (Haredi) Jewish communities—Beis Pinchos located near Stamford Hill, London and Beenstock in Broughton Park, Manchester—which employ much higher proportions of Jews than all the other homes. If these two homes are excluded from this calculation, the percentage of Jewish staff drops to only 2.6 per cent, i.e. approximately sixty-five individuals. Indeed, a large number of Jewish voluntary sector homes have only one Jewish member of staff, if any at all. This obviously has serious implications for the maintenance of a Jewish ethos, which is, after all, the *raison d'être* for the establishment of these homes, and why they attract continued community support. Finding Jewish people willing to work in care homes is extremely difficult:

> Do you need Jewish staff? Preferably, but you can't get hold of them. You can get hold of Jewish social workers, get Jewish people working in day centres—it's a very attractive thing because at the end of the day you go home, you have a social life. In a residential home you're on shift work, it's not an attractive career for the majority of Jewish people, particularly younger people. The salary is reasonable but not enormous in terms of the aspirations of Jewish people. Consequently there is a predominately non-Jewish staff, even in terms of the head of home (social service professional).
>
> There's a national shortage of nurses, particularly so in the elderly sector. But as for Jewish nurses, there aren't any. There are very, very few so that's not even on the

wish list, because we know that's an impossibility ...
We should not kid ourselves, there is not one day going
to be a rush of Jewish people going into nursing (care
home manager).

All the service providers interviewed spoke of similar difficulties, with the exception of those in the strictly Orthodox sector. Here, there is a much greater supply of (particularly) female care staff, although even in these homes around half the staff are non-Jewish. According to one professional working in this sector, these homes prefer staff to be strictly Orthodox or non-Jewish, rather than 'mainstream' Jews. Non-Jewish staff are able to come and work in these homes on the Sabbath, because they are exempt from many of the rules and requirements necessary for keeping this day holy. Non-strictly Orthodox Jews are, according to *halakhah* (Jewish law), still required to keep the Sabbath, even if in practice they may choose not to follow a religious way of life at home. As such, these Jews are unlikely to know the (precise and extremely detailed) Sabbath regulations and thus may infringe religious rules unintentionally.

Several interviewees argued that having very few Jewish staff was not necessarily a problem, and that what really matters is 'what we do, rather than who provides it' (care home manager). This manager argued that obtaining Jewish staff was 'not a burning issue ... we don't go out of our way to attract them, although if we could recruit more, we'd take more'. Another professional argued that having Jewish staff does not necessarily ensure that a home has a Jewish ethos, because there will inevitably be variations in the knowledge, commitment and involvement of these individuals. Nevertheless, because of the shortage of Jewish staff—and arguably especially so where heads of home are not Jewish—

having suitable training schemes in the religious, cultural and social values and traditions of Judaism is extremely important if a Jewish ethos is to be maintained. This is particularly important given the wide variations in prior knowledge about Judaism among new employees.

> There is a big cultural divide between the carers and the cared for. We run a series of lectures, for example on the Holocaust, but many of the staff had either never heard the word 'Holocaust' before, or didn't know what it meant. One staff member at a recent training session thought the Holocaust was a drug for Alzheimer's disease. It is incumbent on us to provide as much training, education input as possible (care home manager).

All of the managers interviewed spoke of having some form of Judaic training for new employees—although these were not always formally part of the induction process—so that they could 'understand the cultural needs of someone in the Jewish community'. Training courses typically involved an understanding and appreciation of kosher food, the various Jewish festivals, the Holocaust, and attitudes and rites involving death and dying. Nevertheless, there were clear variations in the quality of training provided. One manager, for example, admitted that Jewish training was patchy and informal but argued that this was due to the costs involved, while another maintained that 'training has to be measured against the amount of time that can be spared for it and the turnover of staff—if you have a high turnover of staff, you don't get continuity'. Other providers argued that because their core staff had been with the home for many years, knowledge of Judaism was high and thus there was little need for culturally specific training schemes.

While the Judaic training courses provided in some homes were relatively weak or undeveloped, other providers had much more extensive schemes. These latter organizations tended to be those that are larger and thus with higher levels of funding and greater numbers and turnover of staff requiring training. Jewish Care, for example, has a highly respected training scheme to cater for its 1,600 members of staff: all new staff have to complete a comprehensive induction programme, there is an established NVQ (National Vocational Qualification) scheme, and the organization also has the national 'Investors in People' status. Despite the quality of these schemes, some interviewees argued that there is relatively little co-ordination or co-operation between different organizations in the provision of training courses, despite the similarity in needs. Several smaller organizations expressed a clear interest in developing such co-ordinated schemes, or even the creation of specialist itinerant teachers with expertise in methods of Judaic training. Such individuals could travel round the country to help home managers develop innovative ways of encouraging staff to create a Jewish ethos. Interest was also expressed in specialist training schemes for key workers and senior members of staff who could go on intensive training courses to develop further their Jewish knowledge and understanding. Such courses could have the additional advantage of reducing turnover of staff by encouraging a sense of belonging to the particular institution and to the Jewish community as a whole. There may be important lessons and models that can be drawn from Jewish education, in which there are innovative schemes, such as the Jerusalem Fellows and the United Jewish Israel Appeal (UJIA)/Ashdown Fellowships, which are designed to train Jewish educators to the very highest levels. Without a suitable investment in human resources, as well as brick-and-mortar buildings, the care provided to older people in the Jewish community necessarily suffers.

Volunteering

Thousands of Jews carry out unpaid work for the Jewish community every year. For example, the League of Jewish Women (which provides a range of services for both Jews and non-Jews) has some 3,500 volunteers on its books, Jewish Care has 2,500 (although many of these are also under the auspices of the League), while Nightingale House has around 200 (about 60 of whom are regulars). Large organizations will typically have a dedicated volunteer co-ordinator whose job it is to arrange the different array of voluntary activities that take place every week in care homes, day centres and other social care facilities. Activities run by volunteers include the befriending of isolated or lonely older people, providing entertainments in care homes and facilitating visits to places of interest, such as parks, theatres and museums.

Volunteers are the key 'added value' in the provision of services to older people, and indeed throughout the whole of the Jewish voluntary sector. Overall, the government estimates the annual economic gain of volunteering to be worth the equivalent of £12 billion.[8] If this figure is divided per head of population and extrapolated for the approximately 280,000 members of the Jewish community, the economic value would be equivalent to £60 million per year. However, the JPR study by Peter Halfpenny and Margaret Reid, *The Financial Resources of the UK Jewish Voluntary Sector*, estimated the income, expenditure and funds of the Jewish voluntary sector in 1997 to be approximately six times higher than would be expected given the size of the Jewish community relative to the United Kingdom overall.[9] If this figure were also reflected in levels of volunteering, the value to the Jewish community of unpaid staff would be the equivalent of £360 million per year, an amount not far short of the actual total annual expenditure of the UK Jewish voluntary sector. Further research is needed in this area, but the value of volunteering to the Jewish community is certainly immense.

Individuals within the Jewish community volunteer in two broad ways, through governing boards or else in the assistance of direct service provision. Governance involves acting as unpaid lay-leaders in voluntary organizations, typically working with paid staff to determine future policy directions and ensuring standards and ethos. The JPR report by Margaret Harris and Colin Rochester, *Governance in the Jewish Voluntary Sector*, specifically examined governance, noting the high levels of commitment shown by members of Jewish governing bodies.[10] Nevertheless, it also raised problems concerning the general recruitment of volunteers for lay-leadership positions, religious differences that intensify competition for new recruits, a shortage of younger volunteers, and difficulties related to the length of time that certain key individuals stay in their posts.

Volunteers involved in direct service provision for older people provide a range of essential services, such as the delivery of meals-on-wheels, the befriending of individuals in care homes, driving clients to and from facilities or events, assisting in art classes, entertaining clients, or working in shops located in community centres. Such volunteers provide two key elements to Jewish organizations: first, a cost saving to organizations that would otherwise need to employ more paid staff; and, second, the creation of a Jewish atmosphere, a factor that is extremely important given the typically very low Jewish staffing levels. According to one social service professional, 'volunteers bring a very precious element, they create a warm, enthusiastic atmosphere that is the key added ingredient of care'. Volunteers are able to bring the time and commitment that is so important to providing meaning and value for many older people in institutional care, especially given restraints on staffing levels: 'there's a sense in which the staffing ratios only really enable people to do the basic, minimum physical caring, they do not enable people to have that one-to-one relationship, the added value that provides quality of life' (social service professional).

Volunteers are not a free resource. They require ongoing training and development that costs money. Moreover, several interviewees expressed considerable concern that volunteers themselves are becoming increasing elderly and frail, and that younger people are failing to take on these roles.

> Volunteers are an extremely valuable resource, but one of the difficulties we have, and I know other people have had as well, is that sometimes the volunteers are older than the residents. Is it because people just don't have the same sense of communal duty as they used to, or is it that people simply don't have the time? People are working, they've got very busy lives, so to what extent is there going to be a problem in the future recruiting volunteers? ... If you can't get the volunteers, then ultimately you either don't provide the service or you've got more expenses in employing more staff (care home manager).

The Jewish community has a 'proud record of voluntary service which is unequalled' (social service professional). However, there are important concerns as to future trends and whether the next generation of older people will have the same levels of unpaid, voluntary support.

Conclusions

These are difficult times for Jewish voluntary sector care homes, and indeed for private sector suppliers too. In particular, many are facing severe financial pressures as the income supplied by local councils continues to fall short of the actual costs of care. With increasing demands by clients, and the introduction of national minimum standards, these concerns are set to deepen. If central and local government fail to allocate more financial resources to the social care sector, organizations will either have to cut costs and/or services dramatically, or else there will have to be increased communal support. Either way, the *status quo* is not an option.

Closely related to financial questions are strategic issues relating to the future provision of places. As Chapter 4 showed, there are likely to be increased numbers of Jews aged 90+ over the next ten years, and this is the group most likely to need long-term care. Nevertheless, changing government procedures in which clients have to be increasingly frail and infirm to gain state funding is likely to more than offset these demographic changes. Indeed, there are major questions as to the long-term viability of residential care: in the long run, the only forms of institutional care may be in nursing facilities or in homes that cater for EMI clients (see Chapter 9). Demand is also not uniform across the whole country, with different areas having differing requirements: as such, geography matters. Moreover, with the changing expectations of clients, only those homes with suitable modern facilities and high-quality reputations are likely to survive. The introduction of the latest facilities requires large capital investment, the vast bulk of which comes from fundraising within the Jewish community.

Another key strategic issue examined in this chapter relates to human resources. Paid staff—along with the volunteers who support them—are fundamental to the provision of care, so that shortages in quantity and quality create severe problems. Many of the staff working in Jewish voluntary sector homes are clearly of the very highest standard, but with national shortages (especially of registered general nurses) this is a continual problem for many managers. Moreover, the very small number of staff who are Jewish also creates challenges for home managers in terms of creating and maintaining a Jewish ethos, which is, after all, the *raison d'être* for these facilities.

Notes

1. Royal Commission on Long Term Care, 35–6.
2. UK figures from the Royal Commission on Long Term Care, Barnet figures from JPR telephone survey, 2001.
3. 'Crisis at Heathlands', *Jewish Chronicle*, 27 July 2001.
4. 'Heathlands in funds crisis', *Jewish Telegraph*, 27 July 2001.
5. From a survey by Laing and Buisson, reported in 'Counting the losses', *Guardian*, 18 April 2001, and Social Policy Ageing Information Network, *The Underfunding of Social Care and Its Consequences for Older People* (London: Help the Aged 2001).
6. Based on a telephone survey of all the UK Jewish voluntary sector homes.
7. Submission to the King's Fund inquiry by the Association for Residential Care, quoted in Henwood, 99.
8. 'Putting a value on volunteering', *Charity Finance*, June 2001, 24–5.
9. Halfpenny and Reid.
10. Margaret Harris and Colin Rochester, *Governance in the Jewish Voluntary Sector* (London: Institute for Jewish Policy Research 2001).

9 Towards the future of formal long-term care services for older Jewish people

The UK Jewish community has a long and distinguished history of caring for older people. Many of the organizations and institutions that provide services today are able to trace their roots back to the nineteenth century and the foundations of the modern Jewish voluntary sector. Since that time, however, the philosophy and the practicalities of care provision across the whole of the United Kingdom have undergone major changes. Long-term care provision has continually evolved, from the abolition of the Poor Law to the introduction of the Welfare State, from the introduction of community care legislation to the imposition of national minimum standards. Twenty years ago, for example, the average age of residents in care homes was 10–15 years younger than it is today, en-suite rooms were almost unheard of, and residents in nursing homes were likely to live in large multi-bedded wards. Looking to the future, changes are likely to be just as radical and those with the responsibility for strategic planning—and indeed the communities who are the stakeholders of this care—constantly need to be thinking ahead. This chapter aims to help in this process by mapping out future possibilities for the sector. It is not designed to be prescriptive, but rather to provide a starting point for an informed communal debate.

The first part of the chapter considers the current picture of social care provision for older Jews living in the United Kingdom. It reviews some of the factors that will drive future changes—particularly demography, government legislation and societal expectations—and also discusses potential barriers to any improvements sought. The second part considers how these changes may affect the future landscape of service provision, especially domiciliary care and day centres, sheltered housing and institutional care. The third part examines issues relating to innovation, communication and information technology. Ideas discussed include improving connections between different providers, using 'assistive technology' to help people remain independent in their own homes, and the use of information technology both to improve links between (and within) organizations and communities, but also as an educational, vocational and leisure tool for older people. The final part of the chapter sets out the research agenda for long-term planning for older Jewish people. While this book provides a foundation for a strategic understanding of long-term care facilities available for older Jews, specialist research is urgently required to examine issues such as the changing impact of community and family support structures on health and well-being, the effectiveness of different models of institutional care, general and mental health needs, and human resources.

The future of long-term care

Every week thousands of kosher meals-on-wheels are delivered to old and infirm Jews, around 3,000 older Jews attend 21 formal Jewish day centres across the United Kingdom (with thousands more attending Jewish friendship and luncheon clubs), 1,725 reside in sheltered housing accommodation managed by Jewish associations and almost 2,500 live in 36 Jewish voluntary sector care homes. This is in addition to thousands of hours of domiciliary care provided by Jewish social service agencies (assisting people with a range of activities such as bathing, cooking and occupational therapy), thousands of hours of informal care provided to friends and relatives, and semi-formal activities such as synagogue-sponsored bereavement counselling services. Thousands of paid staff and unpaid volunteers are required to run these services. Overall, the extensive range of services and the commitment of individuals, organizations and communities are truly remarkable. Social care provision is a key pillar of the British Jewish community, and its continued maintenance and development are crucial both for those individuals who require its services, and for the future survival of the community itself. Nevertheless, these are changing times and the good work done in the past will be of little value without hard planning decisions about what areas to develop, what to change and what to downgrade or phase out. These decisions need to be based on evidence, rather than on the intuition and suppositions that have too often previously characterized the sector. The starting point in planning future provision involves assessing the principal drivers of change, especially demographic trends, government legislation and future societal expectations. The second stage is an understanding of the potential barriers that face any attempts to plan for the future.

Assessing key drivers of change

Demography. As Chapter 3 showed, the Government Actuary Department (GAD) makes predictions about likely future demographic trends for the United Kingdom population according to age and sex. Over the course of the next sixty years GAD predicts a large increase in both the number of older people and their proportion relative to those of working age: numbers of those aged 75–89 are expected to more than double over the next fifty years, with a peak in 2041–51, followed by a gradual decline or a levelling off; but numbers of those aged 90 or over are expected to increase fourfold, with this pattern expected to be maintained for the foreseeable future. These figures are based on records of births, deaths and marriages, as well as information from the national census held every ten years. Nevertheless, predicting future demographic change is enormously difficult, requiring assumptions about future numbers of births and the likely effects on life expectancies of events such as wars and diseases, as well as changes in living standards and medical technology. All demographic projections are, therefore, prone to error—particularly as they stretch further into the future—and thus should be treated with caution. Moreover, an increase in life expectancies for older people should not be presumed to produce an equivalent rise in the need for long-term care services: dramatic tales of a 'demographic time bomb' should be avoided. Although people are living longer, they are also likely to remain free of long-standing illnesses or disabilities to an older age. Indeed, the major increase in demand for services may come from people with mild or moderate disabilities (who thus require community-based care), rather than those with more serious limitations (who need institutional care).

The demography of the Jewish community is, as Chapter 4 revealed, quite different from the United Kingdom as a whole. In many ways British Jews are demographic pioneers for the rest of the country in terms of having a greater than average proportion of older people. Estimates by the Community Research Unit of the Board of Deputies suggest that the number of Jews aged 75–89 will decline slightly over the next ten years, but that there will an increase of just over 50 per cent in the numbers of those aged 90 or over. Those aged 90+

are statistically most likely to need formal long-term care services, which might suggest a need for an increase in Jewish communal social care provision. Nevertheless, population change—especially when overall numbers are relatively small—is *geographically uneven* with some areas having very different experiences than others. Moreover, the effects of government legislation and changing societal expectations are more than likely to mitigate any changes in Jewish demography, at least in regard to institutional care provision and probably (traditional) sheltered housing as well.

Government legislation. Successive governments have introduced a raft of social care legislation and policy initiatives to modernize services for older people. These have been designed to increase standards, to accommodate a section of the population with an increasing political voice (the so-called 'grey vote'), but also to regulate an industry with spiralling costs: the Royal Commission on Long Term Care established to examine the future funding of long-term care in the United Kingdom estimated the costs in 1995 to be £11 billion, and could (at 1995–6 prices) be as high as £45.3 billion in 2051. In response, the current New Labour government has introduced a series of reforms to shape the future of care delivery. Of particular relevance for the Jewish voluntary sector are changes in the funding of long-term care, the imposition of new regulations and standards for care homes and domiciliary providers, and processes relating to access to care and how local authorities commission their services (see Chapter 3 for details). The government hopes that its reforms will further de-institutionalize the long-term care of older people by promoting people's ability to remain in their homes and thus limit 'avoidable' stays in residential and nursing care homes. It also expects existing and new care homes to improve their services by imposing national minimum standards, which include, for example, requirements for individual bedrooms to be of a minimum size. These standards will inevitably have cost implications for Jewish providers, and for some will require a large investment in bricks-and-mortar infrastructure.

Alongside general government legislation and initiatives for the care sector, there are also elements that are of particular relevance to the Jewish community as an ethnic and religious minority. The Race Relations (Amendment) Act defines Jews as an ethnic group (although the national census does not). As such, Jews are legally entitled to culturally appropriate services. Local authorities can—in theory at least—be legally challenged if they fail to fund the extra costs of providing care in a culturally sensitive manner. Government plans to redefine the relationship between councils and providers—in particular, to allow councils more flexibility in how they pay for services from independent providers—may provide possibilities for Jewish organizations to argue their case for extra funding. Nevertheless, it is also important to note government thinking in regard to 'mainstreaming' services. The aim here is seemingly to provide services in 'inclusive' ways, rather than in environments segregated according to ethnicity or religion. What effect (if any) this will actually have on Jewish providers is unclear.

What is more evident is that, in government publications relating to black and ethnic minority communities' social care needs, Jews are almost completely ignored. The stereotype of Jews being universally financially well off, and having high degrees of communal support, seems to be leading to an assumption that 'they look after their own'. One of the aims of this report has been to challenge such simplistic thinking.

Societal expectations. While it is difficult to predict demographic changes and the effects of government policies, calculating the future needs and wants of society and individual communities is even harder. What does seem inevitable, however, is that the demands and expectations of older people are likely to rise:

> Older people are not going to be as compliant or easily satisfied as in the past. They are no longer a hand-me-down generation, willing to accept what has been given to them. We've bred a new generation of older people who are more educated and self-reliant, more ready to question authority, assert their rights and make their legitimate demands on society.[1]

It is now more than fifty years since the introduction of the Welfare State and people in the United Kingdom have become accustomed to receiving care services from the state that are (or at least people believe they should be) free at the point of delivery, i.e. from a communal pot of money generated from taxation revenues. Over the last twenty years, Conservative and Labour governments have also increasingly portrayed people as consumers of services, with individuals having a 'right' to high-quality care. Indeed, since the general election of 2001, the development of genuinely high-quality public services has become the overriding domestic priority for all of the major UK political parties. Nonetheless, while expectations of formal care services have never been greater, the funding implications of major improvements are more difficult to accept for a public also weaned on calls for lower rates of taxation.

Arguably the only way of predicting future societal expectations for care services is to speak directly to the potential 'market'. JPR's National Survey of British Jewry is intended, in part, to fulfil this function. Analysis in this report of data from the first component of this survey carried out in Leeds paints a picture of the Jewish population in terms of its general and Jewish characteristics, its health as a community, its need for communal services and its attitudes towards future care possibilities (see Chapter 5). Indeed, when directly asked whether they would consider moving to sheltered housing or residential care in the next ten years, over a quarter of Jews aged 75 or over answered 'yes', a quarter said 'no' and the rest did not know. This suggests a future market for these services, but also highlights the difficulties of encouraging people to think about their long-term care needs. Whatever the difficulties of ascertaining people's (realistic) preferences for their long-term care, it is clear that the Jewish community's needs and support structures are changing.

Older Jews currently living in institutional care are likely to have been born between 1900 and 1920. While for a large proportion their parents were immigrants from Eastern Europe, this generation was the first to be born in Britain. They grew up in the bustling inner-city urban environments of the East End of London, the Strangeways and Redbank districts of Manchester or the Glasgow Gorbals. Individuals typically grew up in large, socio-economically deprived families, with parents struggling to find a trade or a business for themselves. Synagogues were the centres of communal activity, and individuals sought to maintain a distinctive personal Jewish identity while also weaving themselves into the fabric of British society. While their parents spoke Yiddish, this was the first generation to have English as its first language. The current generation of older Jews is a last link between pre-war Eastern Europe and the realities of modern urban British life.[2]

TOWARDS THE FUTURE OF FORMAL LONG-TERM CARE SERVICES

The social, cultural, economic, demographic and religious experiences and lifestyles of younger Jews differ in a number of important ways from the generation of Jews currently using long-term care services. First, family sizes have decreased, with individuals having fewer siblings and hence smaller support structures when they are older. Second, there has been a rise in the divorce rate and in single-parent families, as well as an increasing proportion of Jews who never marry.[3] Third, there has been an increasing rate of marriage between Jews and non-Jews, and there are questions as to whether these individuals will want Jewish services when they are older, and whether Jewish organizations will cater for them if they do. Fourth, there are changing social and cultural expectations in terms of individuals' responsibilities to look after their relatives if they can no longer cope on their own. This is especially so given the increasing life expectancies of future generations. Fifth, older Jews in the future are likely to have better pension provision and financial savings for use in their old age. Costs of care are likely to be greater, however, and average figures on socio-economic status for the community will continue to mask those Jews with fewer financial means. Sixth, families are more geographically separated than ever before, thus also threatening the ability of individuals to care directly for relatives on a day-to-day basis. Finally, the Jewish community (or, rather, communities[4]) is far from being socially, culturally or religiously uniform, with different sections of the population varying in their social care needs and in their ability to support themselves. In particular, the strictly Orthodox community—which has experienced rapid demographic growth in recent years—bucks the trend with regard to the rest of British Jewry. This community has a lower overall age profile, much higher birth rate (having more than six children per married couple is common), greater communal support and lower annual income levels, and its members are based in some of the most deprived locations in the country (such as the London borough of Hackney and inner-city Salford).

Potential barriers to change

Despite all the pressures to improve and develop services, there are several important impediments to change that must be recognized. Debates about the future of Jewish formal care services need to be imaginative and forward-thinking, but they also need to be grounded in the realities of what is achievable given finite financial and human resources. There is always a balance between what people would ideally like to see happen, and the limitations of what services can realistically provide. For the Jewish community, there are—as Chapter 8 showed—particular strategic concerns relating to financing services, provision of places and human resources.

Financing services. JPR's report, *Financial Resources of the UK Jewish Voluntary Sector*, calculated that the income in 1997 generated by Jewish organizations in the field of social care was £135 million.[5] New institutional care homes cost millions of pounds to build—the recently opened Jewish Care facility Rosetrees, for example, cost £4.7 million[6]—and average weekly fees for private clients staying in Jewish voluntary sector care homes are around £500 (£445 in residential care, £533 in nursing care). Because social care across the whole of the United Kingdom is a multi-billion pound industry, there is great pressure from central and local government to reduce levels of expenditure.

Jewish organizations across the United Kingdom are reporting major difficulties in continuing to finance their services, given increasingly severe shortfalls from local authorities. For example, councils are typically paying residential and nursing home providers far less than the actual costs of providing full-time care for older people. In conjunction with a general raising of the bar for whether or not local authorities will fund individuals requiring long-term care, several Jewish providers are facing very serious financial problems and indeed a threat to their very survival. While central government imposes national minimum standards, providers are at the mercy of the particular funding procedures and priorities of different local authorities. Thus, where an individual older person lives may determine whether or not they receive long-term care. This is care by postcode.

Provision of places. A second potential barrier to change relates to current and predicted demand from the Jewish community. While numbers of British Jews aged 90+ are expected to increase, the overall community is numerically in decline. In a number of regional communities population decline is likely to result in a gradual tailing off in demand for social care services. As such, it will be of limited value to invest communal money in those services that will only be viable for a short time. Even where Jewish concentrations are higher, there are still questions as to which sections of the community will want to use specifically Jewish services in future years. This will depend partly on the demographic and social structure of the community—for example, levels of assimilation—but also on the quality of services that can be provided. With the increasingly consumerist attitudes of many in the community, questions of religious and cultural preferences could be of less importance than the quality of facilities and services. Such issues are likely to become increasingly important in calculating the future demand for social care services.

Human resources. A third potential barrier to change relates to the availability, and the costs involved, of paid staff and volunteers. Nationally, there are major difficulties for social care providers in recruiting and retaining suitable staff, especially registered nurses (who legally must be employed by nursing and dual registered care homes). This is particularly so in London and the South-east, where costs of living are very high. Even ordinary care staff—who can enter the sector with no previous training—are difficult to recruit because of comparatively low wages, especially following the introduction by the government of the national minimum wage, which has raised the pay of individuals in jobs that had traditionally been lower paid (for example, in the catering and hotel industries).

While general staff recruitment is difficult, obtaining specifically *Jewish* nursing and other care staff is even harder: of the 2,600 people employed in Jewish voluntary sector residential and nursing homes, only 100 are Jewish (or 65 if the two strictly Orthodox homes are excluded from this figure) and most of these are in management or administrative positions. Numbers of staff are hugely important to the quality of care that can be provided. The lack of time for rehabilitation and one-to-one communication (identified in Chapter 7) can be extremely detrimental to the care provided to individual older people in institutional environments.

Planning for the future

The policy changes demanded by demographic trends, government legislation and societal expectations will affect the proportions of care provided in different settings, whether in people's own homes, day centres, sheltered housing or institutional care. Jewish planners need to think imaginatively about what this future social care landscape is likely to look like, particularly in terms of innovative ways of using financial resources from both government and communal sources and possibly also the private sector.

Domiciliary care and day centres

With the thrust of government policy since the 1960s being the maintenance of people's independence in their own homes for as long as possible, the potential for developing domiciliary and day centre services has—in theory, if not necessarily in practice—never been greater. In particular, organizations that can provide temporary respite for older people leaving hospital (either in individuals' own homes or in dedicated settings) may benefit from the changing climate. These organizations have typically found it extremely difficult to obtain local government funding: day centres, for example, are often categorized as 'recreational', rather than as central to maintaining older people's health and well-being. There may be possibilities for taking advantage of government independence grants and changes associated with the Supporting People legislation, which discourage 'unnecessary' institutional care. The real extent of these funds and opportunities is, however, still an open question. This is particularly so given overall concerns about the shortfall in central government funding for social care in general, and the unwillingness of many local authorities to spend the amounts suggested by Statutory Spending Assessments on services for older people (see Chapters 3 and 8).

Direct government bricks-and-mortar investment in communal day centres seems highly unlikely. Nevertheless, there are possibilities for innovative uses of public–voluntary sector partnerships, as, for example, in the development of the Walton Community Care Centre in Giffnock, Glasgow. In a £2.5 million development opened in 1999, the Glasgow community built a brand-new social service day centre alongside new facilities for the Maccabi, which provides educational, sporting and cultural activities. The centre was paid for out of communal funds and a grant from the National Lottery Charities Board (Scotland). One of the organizations working out of the centre is Jewish Care Scotland, which acts in a 'unique partnership' with East Renfrewshire Council to provide social services to the Jewish community. Local authority social workers are based at the Walton Centre, and Jewish Care Scotland is able to provide formal client assessments as well as to deliver statutory services. Jewish Care Scotland benefits from dedicated local authority funding for social work staff, while the council benefits from having culturally sensitive services delivered in first-rate facilities that have been funded by the Jewish community and the National Lottery. There are clearly lessons to be drawn from this partnership, although a lack of communication between social service organizations across the country undermines these possibilities (see later). Moreover, there are also dangers of 'mission drift' if a charity becomes too closely associated with government. If this happens charities or other voluntary organizations can lose their ability to be critical of government, and to distance themselves from the reasons why they were initially established.

The development of world-class social care services and community infrastructure is certainly important to the future health of the UK Jewish voluntary sector, particularly if organizations are to meet rising expectations. Nevertheless, while the trends over the past forty years have been to de-institutionalize care in favour of 'care in the community', problems with this form of provision also need to be recognized. In particular, maintaining people in their own home can mean that they are isolated from the community and may find it extremely difficult coping on their own. While institutional care can lead to a culture of dependency, remaining 'independent' may mean that individuals who are physically and mentally frail are lonely, have little opportunity to make friends, and may be unable to practise their religion fully (they may, for instance, no longer be able to visit their synagogue). If individuals are going to remain longer in their own homes, then the importance of having the best quality domiciliary and day care services cannot be overstated.

Sheltered housing and assisted living

At first glance, one sector that would seem to be able to take advantage of changing government policies, particularly in relation to de-institutionalizing care, is sheltered housing. There is currently, however, little government appetite for funding new sheltered housing schemes (see Chapter 3). The impact of care in the community and changing societal expectations has resulted in the average age of people in sheltered housing increasing markedly. According to one provider, the average age of people in Jewish sheltered housing is now around 85, with schemes changing from being 'stepping stones' to residential and nursing home care, to being ends in themselves: 'we end up with very, very frail people who really should be in residential care.' Local authorities sometimes view maintaining a person in sheltered housing as a cheaper option than funding full-time residential care, and thus may be unwilling to move people despite their needs.

A recent study for the Agudas Israel Housing Association (AIHA) argued that the strictly Orthodox community in Hackney is desperately short of social housing. The report argued that, although strictly Orthodox Jews constitute 10 per cent of Hackney's total population, they occupy only 0.5 per cent of affordable housing units. The greatest need was not for older people's housing, however, but for accommodation for large families. This need reflects the very large family sizes of strictly Orthodox Jews, with AIHA's family homes accommodating an average of just over seven people.[7]

Outside the strictly Orthodox community, the large number of social housing units reflects the boom for affordable housing that followed the Second World War. With state funding for sheltered housing now much harder to obtain, several providers spoke of having obsolete stock located in areas where Jews no longer want to live.

> A lot of the sheltered housing built in the 1960s were bedsits, which aren't really suitable now. The 1960s and 1970s were boom times for sheltered housing, but there are huge problems of older, unwanted stock. Location, location, location is all important, some will go quickly, others are impossible to rent (sheltered housing provider).

Ideally, sheltered housing schemes should move to where Jews are currently living, but with land so expensive (especially in London) and with government funding limitations, this is sometimes impossible. Moreover, with changes in technology, the features built into sheltered housing stock can quickly become obsolete, with problems, for example, obtaining parts for security or warden call systems.

The advantage of sheltered housing schemes is that they allow older people to retain their independence by having their own bedroom, kitchen, living room and bathroom, with residents controlling who enters *their* home and the activities that take place within. Nevertheless, within this environment, there are still wardens available for assistance, and facilities may be explicitly designed to cater for older people's needs (for example, by not having steep stairs and by incorporating specialist baths). Their relative lack of popularity in recent years—at least in terms of the number of newly built constructions—has, in part, been due to people being able to stay longer in their own homes. Older people living in their own homes can make use of aids and adaptations to assist them, such as the addition of seats to showers and the installation of emergency panic buttons in the event of an accident or sudden illness. As such, one interviewee argued that, with care in the community, sheltered housing was increasingly being bypassed as people either stayed in their own home, or else moved directly to a residential or nursing home. Another believed that the community was over-provided for in older people's housing, but desperately short of accommodation for other needy groups of Jews.

> There is a need for Jewish housing in London and it isn't for older people's housing. There's a need for younger people's housing in London and there is none. There's a need for special needs housing in London— Jewish people with mental health related problems, Jewish people with Asperger's syndrome ... I don't think there'll be a need for more sheltered housing, people want to stay in their own homes as long as they want. The lists for sheltered housing are definitely diminishing right down, they're all getting very, very hard to let (sheltered housing provider).

One option considered by some community planners is the development of assisted living (or 'two-and-a-half') schemes.

These models, which have their roots in the Netherlands and Scandinavia, have been adopted by several Jewish communities in the United States.[8] In Kansas City, for example, the Jewish community's care home has been replaced with a $60 million retirement village that offers a range of residences surrounding a central care and leisure centre. It is designed to provide a 'continuum of care', from independent living units to specialist nursing facilities. Within the village there are computer classes, a full gymnasium, cafés, art studios, museum, restaurant, swimming pool and care facilities such as a dental clinic. In Britain the trend over the last two decades or more has been to move away from communal living.[9] Nevertheless, the Joseph Rowntree Foundation has established the Hartrigg Oaks assisted living retirement village (or 'continuing care retirement community' as it calls itself) outside York. The development comprises 152 one- and two-bedroom bungalows with a residential and nursing home at its core. Most of the residents living here are in their late 60s or early 70s.[10]

The idea of assisted living retirement villages is to encourage people to 'age in place' in facilities that promote privacy, autonomy and independence (at least for those that do not require twenty-four-hour nursing care) in a setting specifically and imaginatively designed for the needs and wants of older people. However, these types of facility have been criticized for being too consumerist, with concerns that they lead to a segregation of the community into the rich, who can afford the facilities, and the rest, who cannot. In the United Kingdom, the likelihood of government funding for such facilities is remote, and the costs of such schemes—which necessarily require far more land than residential and nursing homes—will be high. Once again, the issue for planners is to assess the priorities of the community, and whether resources should be used on facilities such as these or, perhaps, on improving domiciliary services and creating world-class day centres.

Institutional care

According to Baroness Greengross (former director general of the charity Age Concern), the future may witness the demise of residential care in its current form and the development of 'genuine community care and extra-care specialist housing'. While there are exciting possibilities for developing non-institutional care provision, care homes are, however, likely to remain at the centre of the Jewish community's provision in the foreseeable future. The responsibility of planners and providers is therefore to continue to improve standards and to review strategically how they deliver their services.

Institutional care is typically perceived in black-and-white terms, either as the way to solve all the problems of isolation and ill-health, or else as facilities that should have been abandoned with the abolition of the Poor Laws. The reality is, however, that as a model of care they have both major strengths and also fundamental drawbacks. Compared with the isolation and the difficulties in coping (both medically and socially) that many older people suffer when they are living in their own home, moving to a long-term care facility can be a huge relief for both themselves and their families. Nevertheless, care homes can also quickly breed high levels of dependency and isolation from friends, family and local communities. Because of limitations in staff numbers, many residents also have a lack of physical and mental stimulation that can be hugely detrimental to their quality of life.

The reality of government legislation and growing expectations from clients and their families means that, whatever the challenges facing institutional providers, reform is inevitable. Nevertheless, such pressures tend to be focused on particular aspects of care, such as the physical construction of care homes (minimum room size, consumer pressure for en-suite facilities etc.) and health and safety requirements. These aspects are certainly important but, if facilities are truly to achieve the highest standard, their development must be above and beyond what is required by the inspection authorities. In particular, there is a need for a debate on the fundamental models of care provision in residential and nursing homes. Despite advances, care in Jewish voluntary sector homes is still too often provided according to a 'top-down' institutional approach, rather than with the full engagement of residents and their families in the running and organization of *their* homes (which were, after all, largely built with community money). The need is to look at care from each individual's perspective. Certainly an increasingly large number of residents in care homes are mentally frail and may suffer from dementia. However, this does not abrogate the need for an active partnership between families and care home staff. Changing an institutional ethos is a notoriously difficult task, but providers seriously need to challenge and re-examine the models of care they offer if they are to remain at the forefront of their industry (see Chapter 7).

Innovation, communication and information technology

In the rapidly changing political, economic and technological environment of social service provision, organizations necessarily have to adapt and update their processes, policies and the ethos by which they provide care. There are now increasing demands by government for organizations to deliver 'best practice' backed up by regular, documented and measurable 'quality assurance'. Pressures on individual service providers have arguably never been greater. At the same time, however, there are also new opportunities to incorporate innovative approaches to care, whether through improving links between different institutions, using 'assistive technology' to allow people to stay longer in their own homes, or making greater use of information technology (IT). While technology should not naively be assumed to be a panacea, it does offer the potential to improve people's lives. IT, for example, can be used to improve communications between and within organizations, and to help strengthen links between providers and users of Jewish services. Moreover, if imaginatively used it has real potential as an educational, vocational and leisure tool for older people, and as an aid to limiting the effects of isolation.

Institutional connections and partnerships

As Chapter 4 reported, there are almost 2,000 financially independent organizations in the UK Jewish voluntary sector (3,700 including subsidiaries and sub-branches).[11] With such a large number of organizations, there are inevitably communication difficulties, especially given the lack of a shared forum for the exchange of ideas following the ending of the Central Council (see Chapter 2), as well as the more usual religious differences, mistrust of organizational motives and personality clashes. As such, finding time to meet and speak with colleagues who have shared interests seems to be increasingly problematic. From interviews with service providers across the United Kingdom, it is clear that there is a lack of communication and a sharing of ideas between the North and the South of the country, as well as between individual organizations located even in the same city.

Opportunities for improving service provision by sharing experiences of best practice are thus being missed.

The largest Jewish social service organization in the United Kingdom is Jewish Care, which annually provides services to 5,000 Jews. Jewish Care operates mainly in the South-east. In the rest of the United Kingdom most towns with a sizeable Jewish population—such as Birmingham, Glasgow, Leeds, Liverpool and Manchester—have their own separate welfare services. The chief executives of regional social service providers do meet on a regular basis, although their contact with voluntary organizations in the South is typically very limited.

> We don't use Jewish Care or Norwood-Ravenswood as much as we should, and that's a two-way process. I would like to see them positively supporting us. We miss out a lot in the regions from their training opportunities, their expertise ... There's a big divide, but both would deny it (regional social service professional).

This interviewee admitted a lack of knowledge of the London organizations, and suggested that this was due to the enormous time and resource pressures required to provide services to the constituent client base: 'you do tend to become quite parochial ... your head gets down, you've got so much to do.' The interviewee argued that there was too little respect for, or acknowledgement of, the achievements of different organizations: 'we should be looking at what each other does, rather than reinventing the wheel—we're not in competition area to area.'

The lack of communication between London and the regions in terms of overall social service provision is clearly of concern, and opportunities such as shared training schemes, staff-exchange initiatives or simply discussions on how to use and adapt to new government legislation are being lost. There are, however, other aspects of Jewish welfare provision that do bring organizations across the United Kingdom together for more regular meetings. There is a national association of Jewish care home providers that organizes a forum for professionals and lay-leaders to discuss shared problems. There is also the National Network for Jewish Social Housing, which similarly provides a forum for exchanging ideas and initiatives. Nevertheless, not all organizations working in these fields make use of these forums, with some institutions being extremely isolationist in their approach to care.

> In most areas of concern we're an organization alone; we don't tend to have joint training sessions with other organizations. Most organizations vigorously defend their autonomy. One can get fairly isolated ... I haven't visited another residential care home in ten years, nor felt the need to (care home manager).

This care home manager believed that there was little point engaging with others employed in similar roles: 'there aren't enough hours in the day, we don't have time to bounce ideas off other people.' There is also the fear that being too closely involved with other organizations will lead to unwanted pressures to merge: 'people will see it as a threat to their autonomy, I can guarantee it ... any talk of sharing anything with an organization brings on a feeling of loss of autonomy and the fear of takeover.' Despite these fears, there are many aspects of formal care provision in which increased co-operation and co-ordination in the delivery of services could be of major benefit, for example, in Manchester.

> To acknowledge that the community is changing, and that what was appropriate 10, 20, 50 years ago will cease to be appropriate from now onwards. It doesn't mean to say that what they're providing isn't good, or that they're not wonderful people for providing it. It means that they're being short-sighted for not adapting to changes (social service provider).

Within Manchester there is a range of Jewish voluntary organizations, including the four care homes (Beenstock, Heathlands, Newlands and Morris Feinmann), the Manchester Jewish Federation (the result of a merger between Jewish Social Services and Manchester Jews' Benevolent Society), Manchester Jewish Community Care (which includes the Nicky Alliance Day Centre), Langdon College, Outreach Community and Residential Services, Manchester Jewish Housing Association, Broughton Park Jewish Housing Association, the Jewish Soup Kitchen and Aguda Community Services. Many of these organizations meet regularly via a 'strategic forum', yet many of those interviewed in the city recognized that increased co-operation and co-ordination of activities could only benefit the community. Several interviewees, for example, expressed frustration that there were three separate organizations providing meals-on-wheels, even though a centralized kosher kitchen could provide significant economies of scale (see also Chapter 4). Moreover, with the increasing financial pressures on organizations, opportunities for sharing costs, such as for in-staff training schemes, are not being taken. In Glasgow the realities of a declining community and diminishing funding resources led to the various social care organizations coming together to build the Walton Community Care Centre. This facility has proved extremely popular with both staff and clients and has been of enormous benefit to the community. The demography of Manchester is clearly very different from that of Glasgow, but the benefits, as well as the potential dangers, of greater co-operation clearly need to be further explored.

Assistive technology

In 1998 the government introduced measures to promote 'lifetime homes', with all newly constructed domestic dwellings required to meet the needs of people who are disabled or infirm. Every new house and flat has to have a level or ramped approach at least 90 cm wide, an entrance door with a minimum 77.5 cm opening, a toilet at the entrance-storey level usable by wheelchair users, corridors wide enough for wheelchair circulation, no change of level on the entrance storey, and switches and sockets between 45 cm and 120 cm from the floor. These changes should make it easier for older people to remain independent if their mobility becomes compromised, for example if they require the use of a wheelchair. Nevertheless, there is also the possibility of introducing a range of technological appliances to make living at home easier, safer and more comfortable, through the creation of so-called 'smart homes'.[12]

Technology can be, and is already being, used in older people's own homes to try to maintain safety and to allow day-to-day tasks to be achieved more easily. Devices already commonplace are external security lights, smoke detectors, timer switches for lights and cooking appliances, alarms to summon help in emergencies and environmental control systems that enable someone to use a remote control to open and close doors and curtains.[13] These technologies may be useful for all frail older people, but there are also adaptations specifically targetted for individuals with dementia. These could include: lights that switch on automatically when a person gets out of bed (particularly useful if they sometimes forget how to get to the toilet); sensors to detect and switch off water taps that are in danger of overflowing sinks or baths; or reminder devices to let a person know if they have left a window open or cooker on when they are leaving their house or flat.[14]

Assistive technologies have the potential of improving people's quality of life by helping them to remain independent. Nevertheless, there are dangers in promoting this type of approach. Technology can be an aid to people with long-term illnesses or disabilities but it should never be seen as a replacement for the human care provided by staff and volunteers. Technology should not be seen as a cost-effective way of preventing people who need institutional or other forms of care from receiving the services they actually require. There are also questions as to whether assistive technologies really are cost-effective and do actually help limit the need for institutional care, or whether they are an unrealistic extra expense for social service departments and voluntary sector organizations that are already overstretched. Nevertheless, they offer exciting possibilities for service providers and users, and certainly require further examination.

Information technology

Interlinked with issues of institutional connections and assistive technologies is the use of information technology (IT). The effective use of IT has the potential not only to improve communication between different organizations, but also to allow service users greater ease in accessing and understanding the gamut of welfare services and information available. For older people themselves, IT can also be used to develop new skills and educational opportunities. This latter point is particularly important given the often negative stereotypes of older people as a 'problem' and a 'burden on society'. At the same time, however, there are dangers in overestimating the value of IT, with the crash in the dot.com sector being just one example.

As Chapter 6 discussed, the process of choosing a care home for oneself or a relative can be complex and traumatic, with decisions having to be made in often a very short space of time. Within London and the South-east, Jewish Care runs a social work help desk that provides clients with information on the wide range of options, from domiciliary care to residency in a nursing home. In the regions, no organization has such a comprehensive range of services, although most sizeable communities do have dedicated Jewish social service agencies. Nevertheless, the option of using IT to create, for example, a 'one-stop' informational website—or a series of interconnected sites for different geographical areas—is something that could usefully be further explored. Many organizations were extremely positive about such ideas, although one in particular argued strongly that this would be a waste of time and resources, and that communal effort should be concentrated on other more immediate issues.

In previous years, the Central Council published the *Directory of Jewish Social Services*, which provided a brief summary and contact details for a range of Jewish voluntary sector organizations.[15] However, while this directory (which is currently being updated by the Board of Deputies of British Jews) largely provided information to service providers, service users were—despite the intentions of its creators—unlikely to know of its existence. In Manchester, Jewish voluntary organizations have created a shared calendar of events to avoid similar activities being provided on the same day. However, while providers now know what events are being provided, service users still do not. Some form of 'one-stop' community website that could be accessed by the local Jewish community could be extremely valuable in this regard, providing joined-up communal information. Such a site could perhaps have information about community events, facilities available, different care options, processes of obtaining a place at a care home, key financial information, care home brochures, annual reports of social service providers, literature on caring for individuals with particular conditions, contacts for people in similar situations, general advice lines, opportunities for further reading and how to proceed with enquiries and concerns. Such a site would not be able to detail fully the incredibly complex mechanisms of the UK system of care, but it would provide a starting point for potential users to understand some of the options and the realities of care.

One private care home that established a website has already attracted considerable interest: 'I did it six or seven months ago because I like to be ahead of the game, but I thought we wouldn't get enquiries on it for three or four years. We receive two or three enquiries on that website every week.' Nevertheless, this manager also warned of the dangers of having too many sites providing information. There are already at least two commercial Jewish websites (Totallyjewish.com and Jewish.co.uk), plus a whole host of communal organizations with websites, such as the Board of Deputies (www.bod.org.uk) and Brijnet (www.brijnet.org).

> I think that web presence on the Net is crucial, but as with everything else on the web, multiplicity and loads of people doing a similar thing is very, very unhelpful. I think at the end of the day the community needs one host, and only one host, and that's a problem because everybody's vying for it. Certainly the information

> needs to be present on the web, there's no question about that. It will happen. It needs to happen (care home manager).

One of the problems, of course, with the use of IT is that many older people will not have access to computers, or may be too frail or infirm to make use of them. As Chapter 4 pointed out, the average age of clients in Jewish institutional care homes in London is almost 90, with a sizeable percentage categorized as elderly mentally infirm (EMI), with conditions such as Alzheimer's disease or other forms of dementia. There are certainly considerable barriers and challenges. However, with the government's commitment to overcoming the 'digital divide'—the gap between those making use of new technologies such as the Internet and those who are not—there are also exciting possibilities. The charity British ORT has established a beginner's computer course for those aged over 60, while Age Resource (a programme run by Age Concern) has developed similar 'taster' sessions for older people across the United Kingdom. Moreover, Age Resource is also working with pilot schemes to introduce computers into care homes, with some very positive initial results.

Some Jewish residential and nursing homes have already begun introducing computer terminals, while other providers spoke of having similar plans. One care home manager argued that they could be extremely useful for mentally active residents, providing an opportunity for them to communicate with relatives and friends and as an educational tool: 'it would make the blow from losing physical abilities much softer. If I had three computers, I'd have a queue.' Another social service provider argued: 'We've got members in their 90s who'd love to access a website or surf the Internet ... people often underestimate our service users, some of them are so skilled and interested in what's going on in the outside world.' Research by Age Concern and Microsoft suggests that 4 million people in the United Kingdom over the age of fifty have their own computers, with a further 600,000 using machines in libraries and colleges. The most popular activities are correspondence and e-mail, followed by surfing the web.[16] According to the Royal Commission on Long Term Care:

> Television, radio and the Internet are not the sole domain of the young—they can enrich the lives of all of us. Older minds need stimulation as much as their bodies may come to need care. The role of depression and social exclusion in diminishing the overall well-being of older people is an important issue. Technology can and will help.[17]

Despite such positive thinking, some care home managers believed that their residents were just too frail to make use of such facilities, as one explained: 'Most residents have to be bribed even to go out in the garden.' Despite the difficulties, it is evident that future generations are going to be increasingly demanding in terms of the technological facilities available for them—whether the use of the Internet or innovative aids and adaptations—and this requires forward planning.

> I'm sure in the future that, just as now en-suites are pretty much standard, in the very near future, people will need a computer in their bedroom, flush to the wall. I don't accept that it can't provide stimulation for different levels of confusion, because you look at a two-year-old, at three-year-olds banging mouses and doing

things, and in many ways a 90-year-old with dementia is very similar to a two-year-old ... With the right level of support, it's a very interesting way of opening up the world to older people (care home manager).

The research agenda for the long-term planning of formal care services

This book has offered a foundation text to aid in the planning of long-term care facilities for older Jewish people. It offers a 'level playing field' of information to help providers—and the individuals and communities who use Jewish services—plan effectively for the future. By piecing together the jigsaw of different elements required for effective strategic planning—including an understanding of demography, government legislation, societal expectations and barriers to change—effective decision-making can be enhanced. Nevertheless, delivering care services in the twenty-first century will be increasingly complex, and some of the issues signposted in this report—and that are also dealt with in JPR's National Survey of British Jewry (see Preface)—need to be examined in more depth. In particular, there are five pressing areas of research: the changing role of communal and inter-generational support structures; the effectiveness of different models of institutional care; general health issues specific to the Jewish community; mental health needs; and human resources.

The first area of research relates to the major changes taking place both in the overall structure of the Jewish community and in the constitution of individual families. These changes are set to have a massive impact on the nature of care services, the extent to which family support for older people will be available, and the future needs and wants of the community. Research is urgently needed into the likely impact of these changes for care providers. Moreover, given problems of institutionalization within care home environments and the potential isolation of those still living at home—together with limitations in staff numbers and a potential decline in family support structures—the need for community involvement in social care services has never been greater. There is massive potential to improve the day-to-day lives of older people through increasing communal and inter-generational family support. How the untapped potential of communities can be transferred to the different social care environments needs to be examined.

A second area for research involves an examination of different models of care provided in institutional environments. This report identified some of the major problems of care home living, such as processes of dependency, lack of mental stimulation and limits to user involvement and empowerment. Nevertheless, some care homes are better than others, and an examination of models of care—both in this country and abroad—that are most successful in improving people's day-to-day lives would be of enormous benefit to the community. Such research could also help counter some of the problems of organizational isolation that have been identified.

A third area for further work concerns the particular health needs and experiences of older Jewish people. Ethnic minority communities are known to have different mortality rates for a range of conditions and diseases than the rest of the population. The data from the JPR survey of Leeds (see Chapter 5) shows how older (and indeed younger) Jews have higher self-reported rates of asthma and diabetes. Further research is needed to determine whether these differences relate simply to better health awareness amongst this community or higher prevalence rates. Are the rates in Leeds similar to other Jewish communities in the United Kingdom and abroad and, if not, what factors might explain any geographical variations? Are there differences in rates of illnesses other than asthma and diabetes for Jews compared with the wider society?

A fourth area—and one that has largely been ignored in relation to people across all age groups—relates specifically to mental health needs. With regard to older people, the realities of an ageing population mean that there are likely to be larger numbers of people with (at least some) mental frailties. Already half of all residents in care homes are diagnosed as having cognitive functioning problems, and such clients require specialized care and support. Some Jewish organizations are at the cutting edge of providing facilities to those with dementia. For example, some Jewish residential and nursing homes have developed highly specialized schemes, set in purpose-built environments, which have greatly enhanced care standards. Nevertheless, these schemes are in their infancy and have yet to extend across the whole sector. The role of religion, culture and ethnicity in the care of people with dementia is something that could usefully be explored. There are also wider questions relating to how providers can develop their mental health services, and how to extend principles of user involvement and empowerment to those with cognitive functioning problems.

A fifth area of further investigation that is needed by the community concerns human resources. Limitations in staff numbers and volunteers are an enormous problem, both throughout the United Kingdom generally and specifically in the Jewish voluntary sector. Moreover, attracting *Jewish* members of staff is even more difficult, given the current relatively low level of interest in the community in working in the social care sector. Research into innovative ways of recruiting and retaining staff could also have a tremendous impact on people's day-to-day experiences of Jewish services.

In conclusion

This book has highlighted some of the strengths and weaknesses of long-term care facilities provided for older British Jews. In many ways Jewish communal providers are among the very best in the country, with systems of care that are a model to other Jewish and minority communities across the world. Nonetheless, providers are in an environment of ever-higher expectations and demanding government legislation. Developing care services that can match the aspirations of communities in the twenty-first century requires imagination, foresight and a willingness to take brave decisions. At the same time, improvements are not cost-free, and individuals and communities need to determine their priorities and their willingness (either through taxation, increased contributions to voluntary organizations or payments to private bodies) to pay for services. Individuals also need to decide on their own responsibilities for paying for, and actively involving themselves in, the care of relatives and of older people in the community more widely. This book is designed to encourage these debates.

Notes

1 Baroness Greengross, quoted in David Brindle, 'Grey demands set to rise', *Guardian*, 8 November 2000.

2 For a discussion of this in the American context, see Allen

Glicksman, 'Saying goodbye to my Yiddishe mama', *Reconstructionist*, vol. 64, no. 2, 2000, 38–47.
3 For an interesting discussion on the effect of childlessness on social support networks, see G. Clare Wenger, Anne Scott and Nerys Patterson, 'How important is parenthood? Childlessness and support in old age in England', *Ageing and Society*, vol. 20, 2000, 161–82.
4 See Commission on Representation of the Interests of the British Jewish Community.
5 Halfpenny and Reid.
6 Judith Zerdin, 'Jewish Care puts finishing touches to "home from home" for elderly', *Jewish Chronicle*, 20 April 2001.
7 Holman.
8 Martin Valins and Derek Salter, *Futurecare: New Directions in Planning Health and Care Environments* (Oxford: Blackwell Science 1996). See also United Jewish Communities, *The Continuum of Care in the 21st Century, An Action Guide: Helping Federations Meet the Needs of Our Jewish Elderly* (Washington D.C.: United Jewish Communities 2001).
9 Heywood, Oldman and Means.
10 Julienne Hanson, 'From "special needs" to "lifestyle choices": articulating the demand for "third age" housing', in Sheila M. Peace and Caroline Holland (eds), *Inclusive Housing in an Ageing Society: Innovative Approaches* (Bristol: Policy Press 2001), 29–53. See also Judith Phillips, Miriam Bernard, Simon Biggs and Paul Kingston, 'Retirement communities in Britain: a "third way" for the third age?', in Peace and Holland (eds), 189–213.
11 Halfpenny and Reid.
12 Heywood, Oldman and Means.
13 Ibid.; Malcolm J. Fisk, 'The implications of smart home technologies', in Peace and Holland (eds), 101–24; Royal Commission on Long Term Care.
14 Mary Marshall, 'Dementia and technology', in Peace and Holland (eds), 125–43.

15 Central Council for Jewish Community Services, *Directory of Jewish Social Services* (London: Central Council for Jewish Community Services 1997).
16 Karen Bowerman, 'Silver surfers boom', *BBC News Online*, 20 May 2000.
17 The Royal Commission on Long Term Care, 3.

Bibliography

Alderman, Geoffrey (1992), *Modern British Jewry* (Oxford: Clarendon Press).

Audit Commission (1998), *Home Alone: The Role of Housing in Community Care* (London: Audit Commission Publications).

Bauld, Linda, John Chesterman and Ken Judge (2000), 'Measuring satisfaction with social care amongst older service users: issues from the literature', *Health and Social Care*, vol. 8, 316–24.

Bebbington, Andrew and Adelina Comas-Herrera (2000), *Healthy Life Expectancy: Trends to 1998, and the Implications for Long Term Care Costs*, PSSRU Discussion Paper 1695 (London School of Economics), December.

Bebbington, Andrew, Robin Darton, Royston Bartholomew and Ann Netten (2000), *Survey of Admissions to Residential and Nursing Home Care: Final Report of the 42 Month Follow Up*, PSSRU Discussion Paper 1675 (London School of Economics), August.

Blakemore, Kenneth and Margaret Boneham (1994), *Age, Race and Ethnicity: A Comparative Approach* (Buckingham: Open University Press).

Bland, Rosemary (ed.) (1996), *Developing Services for Older People and Their Families* (London and Bristol, PA: Jessica Kingsley).

—— (1999), 'Independence, privacy and risk: two contrasting approaches to residential care for older people', *Ageing and Society*, vol. 19, 539–60.

Blunden, Roger (1998), *Terms of Engagement: Engaging Older People in the Development of Community Services* (London: King's Fund).

Board of Deputies of British Jews (1999), *Report on Community Statistics for 1999* (London: Board of Deputies of British Jews).
—— (2000), *Report on Community Statistics for 2000* (London: Board of Deputies of British Jews).
Bowerman, Karen (2000), 'Silver surfers boom', *BBC News Online*, 20 May.
Brindle, David (2000), 'Grey demands set to rise', *Guardian*, 8 November.
Carlowe, Melvyn (1996), 'Social Service', in Stephen Massil (ed.), *The Jewish Year Book 1996* (London: Vallentine Mitchell), xlii–li.
Central Council for Jewish Community Services (1997), *Directory of Jewish Social Services* (London: Central Council for Jewish Community Services).
Collins, Kenneth (1990), *Second City Jewry* (Glasgow: Scottish Jewish Archives).
Commission on Representation of the Interests of the British Jewish Community (2000), *A Community of Communities: Report of the Commission on Representation of the Interests of the British Jewish Community* (London: Institute for Jewish Policy Research).
'Counting the losses' (2001), *Guardian*, 18 April.
'Crisis at Heathlands' (2001), *Jewish Chronicle*, 27 July.
Curran, Julie (1996), 'The evolution of daycare services for people with dementia', in Rosemary Bland (ed.), *Developing Services for Older People and Their Families* (London and Bristol, PA: Jessica Kingsley), 112–28.
Department of Health (1996), *Moving into a Care Home: Things You Need to Know* (London: Department of Health Publications).
—— (1998), *Modernising Social Services: Promoting Independence, Improving Protection, Raising Standards*,

Cm 4169 (London: Stationery Office).

—— (1999), *Fit for the Future? National Required Standards for Residential and Nursing Homes for Older People*, Consultation Document (London: Department of Health Publications).

—— (2000), *Community Care Statistics 1999: Residential Personal Social Services for Adults, England*, Statistical Bulletin 2000/2 (London: Department of Health Publications).

—— (2000), *The NHS Plan: A Plan for Investment; A Plan for Reform*, Cm 4818-I (London: Stationery Office).

—— (2000), *The NHS Plan: The Government's Response to the Royal Commission on Long Term Care*, Cm 4818-II (London: Stationery Office).

—— (2001), *Building Capacity and Partnership in Care: An Agreement between the Statutory and the Independent Social Care, Health Care and Housing Sectors* (London: Department of Health Publications).

—— (2001), *Domiciliary Care: National Minimum Standards Regulations. Consultation Document* (London: Department of Health Publications).

—— (2001), *Fair Access to Care Services: Policy Guidance*, Consultation Draft (London: Department of Health Publications).

—— (2001), 'Health survey for England: The health of older people—First release tables', press release, 29 June 2001.

—— (2001), *Care Homes for Older People: National Minimum Standards* (London: Stationery Office).

—— (2001), *National Service Framework for Older People* (London: Department of Health Publications).

Department of Health/Department of the Environment, Transport and the Regions (2001), *Better Care, Higher Standards: A Charter for Long Term Care* (London:

Department of Health Publications).

Department of the Environment, Transport and the Regions (2001), *Supporting People: Policy into Practice* (London: Department of the Environment, Transport and the Regions).

Evandrou, Maria (ed.) (1997), *Baby Boomers: Ageing into the 21st Century* (London: Age Concern).

Fernàndez-Ballesteros, Rocío, Maria Zamarron and Miguel Angel Ruíz, (2001), 'The contribution of socio-demographic and psychosocial factors to life satisfaction', *Ageing and Society*, vol. 21, 25–43.

Fisk, Malcolm J. (2001), 'The implications of smart home technologies', in Sheila M. Peace and Caroline Holland (eds), *Inclusive Housing in an Ageing Society: Innovative Approaches* (Bristol: Policy Press), 101–24.

Foucault, Michel (1967), *Madness and Civilisation* (London: Routledge).

—— (1977), *Discipline and Punish: The Birth of the Prison* (London: Penguin).

Francis, Doris (1984), *Will You Still Need Me, Will You Still Feed Me, When I'm 84?* (Bloomington: Indiana University Press).

Gartner, Lloyd (1973), *The Jewish Immigrant in England 1870–1914* (London: Simon Publications).

Gilman, Sander L. (2002), 'Private knowledge', *Patterns of Prejudice*, vol. 36, no. 1, 5–16.

Glicksman, Allen (2000), 'Saying goodbye to my Yiddishe mama', *Reconstructionist*, vol. 64, no. 2, 38–47.

Goddard, Eileen and David Savage (1994), *People Aged 65 and Over: A Study Carried Out on Behalf of the Department of Health as Part of the 1991 General Household Survey* (London: HMSO).

Goffman, Erving (1961), *Asylums: Essays on the Social*

Situation of Mental Patients and Other Inmates (London: Penguin).

Gracie, David and John Vincent (1998), 'Progress report: religion and old age', *Ageing and Society*, vol. 18, 101–10.

Halfpenny, Peter and Margaret Reid (2000), *The Financial Resources of the UK Jewish Voluntary Sector* (London: Institute for Jewish Policy Research).

Hanson, Julienne (2001), 'From "special needs" to "lifestyle choices": articulating the demand for "third age" housing', in Sheila M. Peace and Caroline Holland (eds), *Inclusive Housing in an Ageing Society: Innovative Approaches* (Bristol: Policy Press), 29–53.

Harper, Sarah (2000), 'Ageing update: ageing 2000—questions for the 21st century', *Ageing and Society*, vol. 20, 111–22.

Harris, Margaret and Colin Rochester (2001), *Governance in the Jewish Voluntary Sector* (London: Institute for Jewish Policy Research).

'Heathlands in funds crisis' (2001), *Jewish Telegraph*, 27 July.

Henwood, Melanie (2001), *Future Imperfect? Report of the King's Fund Care and Support Inquiry* (London: King's Fund).

Heywood, Francis, Christine Oldman and Robin Means (2002), *Housing and Home in Later Life* (Buckingham: Open University Press).

Hödl, Klaus (2002), 'The black body and the Jewish body: a comparison of medical images', *Patterns of Prejudice*, vol. 36, no. 1, 17–34.

Holman, Christine (2001), *Orthodox Jewish Housing Need in Stamford Hill* (London: Agudas Israel Housing Association).

Home Office/Department of Health (2000), *No Secrets: Guidance on Developing and Implementing Multi-agency Policies and Procedures to Protect Vulnerable Adults from Abuse* (London: Home Office).

Jimack, Michael (1992), *Residential Care and Nursing Provision for the Elderly in the Greater London Jewish Community* (London: Jewish Care).

Kendall, Jeremy (2000), *The Third Sector and Social Care for Older People in England: Towards an Explanation of Its Contrasting Contributions in Residential Care, Domiciliary Care and Day Care*, Civil Society Working Paper 8 (London: PSSRU, London School of Economics).

—— and Martin Knapp (1996), *The Voluntary Sector in the UK* (Manchester: Manchester University Press).

King, Imogene (1981), *A Theory for Nursing: System, Concept, Process* (New York: Wiley).

Klein, Paul (2001), 'Painful side of visiting the aged', *Jewish Chronicle*, letters page, 21 September.

Kosmin, Barry (1997), 'Foreword', in Margaret Harris, *The Jewish Voluntary Sector in the United Kingdom: Its Role and Its Future* (London: Institute for Jewish Policy Research).

—— (1999), *Ethnic and Religious Questions in the 2001 UK Census of Population: Policy Recommendations* (London: Institute for Jewish Policy Research).

Krausz, Ernest (1964), *Leeds Jewry: Its History and Social Structure* (Cambridge: Jewish Historical Society of England).

Langer, Ellen (1989), *Mindfulness: Choice and Control in Everyday Life* (London: Harvill).

Macpherson, William (1999), *The Stephen Lawrence Inquiry: Report of an Inquiry by Sir William Macpherson of Cluny* (London: Stationery Office).

Marshall, Mary (2001), 'Dementia and technology', in Sheila M. Peace and Caroline Holland (eds), *Inclusive Housing in an Ageing Society: Innovative Approaches* (Bristol: Policy Press), 125–43.

Massil, Stephen (ed.) (2001), *The Jewish Year Book 2001* (London: Vallentine Mitchell).

Means, Robin (2001), 'Lessons from the history of long-term care for older people', in Janice Robinson (ed.), *Towards a New Social Compact for Care in Old Age* (London: King's Fund), 9–27.

—— and Randall Smith (1998), *From Poor Law to Community Law: The Development of Welfare Services for Elderly People 1939–1971* (Bristol: Policy Press).

Miller, Stephen, Marlena Schmool and Antony Lerman (1996), *Social and Political Attitudes of British Jews: Some Key Findings of the JPR Survey* (London: Institute for Jewish Policy Research).

Milne, Alison, Eleni Hatzidimitriadou, Christina Chryssanthopoulou and Tom Owen (2001), *Caring in Later Life: Reviewing the Role of Older Carers* (London: Help the Aged).

Mullan, Phil (2000), *The Imaginary Time Bomb: Why an Ageing Population Is Not a Social Problem* (London: I. B. Tauris).

Neuberger, Julia (1998), 'Foreword', in Alison Turnbull (ed.), *Home from Home: Your Guide to Choosing a Care Home* (London: King's Fund).

Office for National Statistics (2000), *Living in Britain: Results from the 1998 General Household Survey* (London: Stationery Office).

Office of Fair Trading (1998), *Older People as Consumers in Care Homes* (London: Office of Fair Trading).

Oldman, Christine and Deborah Quilgars (1999), 'The last resort? Revisiting ideas about older people's living arrangements', *Ageing and Society*, vol. 19, 363–84.

Orem, Dorothea (1980), *Nursing Concepts for Practice* (New York: McGraw).

Patel, Naina (1999), 'Black and minority ethnic elderly: perspectives on long-term care', in Royal Commission on

Long Term Care, *With Respect to Old Age: Long Term Care—Rights and Responsibilities* (London: Stationery Office), Research Volume 1.

Peace, Sheila M., Leonie Kellaher and Dianne Willcocks (1997), *Re-evaluating Residential Care* (Buckingham: Open University Press).

Peace, Sheila M. and Caroline Holland (eds) (2001), *Inclusive Housing in an Ageing Society: Innovative Approaches* (Bristol: Policy Press).

Phillips, Judith, Miriam Bernard, Simon Biggs and Paul Kingston (2001), 'Retirement communities in Britain: a "third way" for the third age?', in Sheila M. Peace and Caroline Holland (eds), *Inclusive Housing in an Ageing Society: Innovative Approaches* (Bristol: Policy Press), 189–213.

Phillipson, Chris and Neil Thompson (1996), 'The social construction of old age: new perspectives on the theory and practice of social work with older people', in Rosemary Bland (ed.), *Developing Services for Older People and Their Families* (London and Bristol, PA: Jessica Kingsley), 13–25.

Philo, Chris and Hester Parr (2000), 'Institutional geographies: introductory remarks', *Geoforum*, vol. 31, 513–21.

Pollins, Henry (1982), *Economic History of the Jews in England* (London: Associated University Presses).

Pritchard, Jacki (2001), *Male Victims of Elder Abuse: Their Experiences and Needs* (London: Jessica Kingsley).

'Putting a value on volunteering' (2001), *Charity Finance*, June.

Raynes, Norma (1998), 'Involving residents in quality specification', *Ageing and Society*, vol. 18, 65–78.

Roberts, Emilie, Janice Robinson and Linda Seymour (2002),

Old Habits Die Hard: Tackling Age Discrimination in Health and Social Care (London: King's Fund).

Roper, Nancy, Winifred Logan and Alison Tierney (1990), *The Elements of Nursing* (Edinburgh: Churchill Livingstone).

Roy, Callista (1984), *Introduction to Nursing: An Adaptation Model* (London: Prentice-Hall).

Royal Commission on Long Term Care (1999), *With Respect to Old Age: Long Term Care—Rights and Responsibilities* (London: Stationery Office).

Samuel, Elaine and Charlotte Pearson (1999), 'The Jewish community of Greater Glasgow: population and residential patterns', Department of Social Policy, University of Edinburgh.

Schlesinger, Ernest (2000), *Grant-making Trusts in the Jewish Voluntary Sector* (London: Institute for Jewish Policy Research).

Schmool, Marlena and Frances Cohen (1998), *A Profile of British Jewry: Patterns and Trends at the Turn of a Century* (London: Board of Deputies of British Jews).

Sidell, Moyra (1995), *Health in Old Age: Myth, Mystery and Management* (Buckingham: Open University Press).

Social Policy Ageing Information Network (2001), *The Underfunding of Social Care and Its Consequences for Older People* (London: Help the Aged).

Social Services Inspectorate (1998), *They Look After Their Own, Don't They?* (London: Department of Health Publications).

Steverink, Nardi (2001), 'When and why frail elderly people give up independent living: The Netherlands as an example', *Ageing and Society*, vol. 21, 45–69.

Stuckey, Jon (2001), 'Blessed assurance: the role of religion and spirituality in Alzheimer's disease caregiving and other significant life events', *Journal of Ageing Studies*, vol. 15, 69–84.

Thane, Pat (2000), *Old Age in English History: Past Experiences, Present Issues* (Oxford: Oxford University Press).

Townsend, Peter (1962), *The Last Refuge* (London: Routledge and Kegan Paul).

—— (1981), 'The structured dependency of the elderly: the creation of social policy in the twentieth century', *Ageing and Society*, vol. 1, 5–28.

Turnbull, Alison (ed.) (1998), *Home from Home: Your Guide to Choosing a Care Home* (London: King's Fund).

Twigg, Julia (2000), *Bathing—The Body and Community Care* (London: Routledge).

United Jewish Communities (2001), *The Continuum of Care in the 21st Century, An Action Guide: Helping Federations Meet the Needs of Our Jewish Elderly* (Washington D.C.: United Jewish Communities).

United Synagogue (2001), *Care Matters: A Directory of Information for Care Providers in the United Synagogue* (London: United Synagogue).

Valins, Martin and Derek Salter (1996), *Futurecare: New Directions in Planning Health and Care Environments* (Oxford: Blackwell Science).

Valins, Oliver (1999), 'Identity, Space and Boundaries: Ultra-Orthodox Judaism in Contemporary Britain', Ph.D. thesis, University of Glasgow.

—— (2000), 'Institutionalised religion: sacred texts and Jewish spatial practice', *Geoforum*, vol. 31, 575–86.

——, Barry Kosmin and Jacqueline Goldberg (2001), *The Future of Jewish Schooling in the United Kingdom: A Strategic Assessment of a Faith-based Provision of Primary and Secondary School Education* (London: Institute for Jewish Policy Research).

Warnes, Anthony (1996), 'The demography of old age: panic versus reality', in Rosemary Bland (ed.), *Developing Services for Older People and Their Families* (London and Bristol, PA: Jessica Kingsley), 26–42.

Waterman, Stanley and Barry Kosmin (1986), *British Jewry in the Eighties: A Statistical and Geographical Study* (London: Board of Deputies of British Jews).

—— (1986), 'Mapping an unenumerated ethnic population: Jews in London', *Ethnic and Racial Studies*, vol. 9, 484–501.

Wenger, G. Clare, Anne Scott and Nerys Patterson (2000), 'How important is parenthood? Childlessness and support in old age in England', *Ageing and Society*, vol. 20, 161–82.

Wolfenden, John (1978), *The Future of Voluntary Organisations* (London: Croom Helm).

Yee, Lydia and Barry Mussenden (2001), *From Lip Service to Real Service: The Report of the First Phase of a Project to Assist Councils with Social Services Responsibilities to Develop Services for Black Older People* (London: Department of Health Publications).

Zborowski, Mark and Elizabeth Herzog (1952), *Life Is with People: The Culture of the Shtetl* (New York: Schocken Books).

Zerdin, Judith (2001), 'Jewish Care puts finishing touches to "home from home" for elderly', *Jewish Chronicle*, 20 April.

Index

access to services 48, 53–9, 193
activities 140, 153, 161
Age Concern 118, 152, 207, 217–18
age of residents 86, 174, 189, 203
Age Resource (*see also* Age Concern) 217
ageing in place 206
ageism 150
Aguda Community Services 212
Agudas Israel Housing Association (AIHA) 80, 84, 122, 203–4
aids and adaptations 205, 218
alcohol 104
almshouses 10, 14, 26
Alwoodley, Leeds 95, 108
Alzheimer's disease *see* dementia
antisemitism (*see also* Holocaust, pogroms) 22, 128–9
anxiety 102–3
aromatherapy 140
arthritis 135
arts and crafts 137–8, 146, 155, 184
Ashdown Fellowships 182

Ashkenazi Jews' Hospital 26
Asperger's syndrome 205
assimilation 69, 75, 114, 173, 175, 197, 199
assisted living 205–7
assistive technology 209, 213–14
Association of Jewish Friendship Clubs 76
Association of Jewish Refugees 77
asthma 102–3, 109, 220
Audit Commission 46
autoimmune diseases 103

Barnet, London borough of 70, 84, 87, 119, 122, 167–8, 174
Barthel score 47
baths/bathing 16, 38, 41–2, 44, 50, 78–9, 105, 109, 136–7, 139, 144, 153, 162, 205
Beenstock 123, 179, 212
Beis Pinchos 84, 179
bereavement counselling 76, 191
best value (*see also* quality assurance) 46, 56
Better Care, Higher Standards 19, 55

Bevan, Aneurin 14
biblical period 9, 20
Birmingham 81, 210
Bnai Brith JBG 80
Board of Deputies of British Jews 4, 66, 73, 88, 94, 192, 215–16
Board of Guardians for the Relief of the Jewish Poor (*see also* Jewish Welfare Board) 26
Booth 14
Bournemouth 81
Bread and Coals Society 26
Brent, London borough of 84
Brighton and Hove Jewish Home (*see also* Jewish Care) 27
Brijnet 216
British ORT 217
British Tay-Sachs Association (*see also* Jewish Care) 27
brochures 118, 120, 216
Brodetsky school 95
Broughton Park Jewish Housing Association 212
Broughton Park, Manchester 70, 126, 179, 198
Building Capacity and Partnership in Care 56

Cainer, Joy 171
cancer 47, 103
Cardiff 81, 84
care by postcode 169–70, 199

Care Standards Act 19, 51, 53, 156
Central Council 27–8, 209, 215
central Orthodox 67, 69, 95, 99
Charity Commission 175
chiropody 42, 78
choice 13, 15, 18, 51, 113–31, 138, 142, 152, 160, 215; geographical location 121–3; Jewish ethos 126–9; social environment and standards 124–6
church 9, 10, 13–14
cigarettes 104
Clapham, South London 122
cognitive functioning difficulties (*see also* dementia) 48, 86, 138
commissioning services 53–9, 193
communication, lack of 202, 209–13
community care (*see also* domiciliary care) 16–18, 28, 46, 202
computers (*see also* information technology) 99, 146, 217–19
Conservative party/ government 13, 17, 195
consumerism *see* market
continuum of care 206
cost ceilings 172
Crohn's disease 103
Cromwell, Oliver 25

INDEX

cultural appropriateness 56–7, 113, 127, 145, 168–9, 194, 202

day centres 4, 40–4, 59, 75–6, 89, 96, 106, 171–2, 183–4, 190, 201–3, 207
death rituals 24–5, 52, 148, 181
de-institutionalization (*see also* institutionalization, independence) 18, 193, 202–3
dementia (*see also* cognitive functioning difficulties) 3, 43–4, 78–9, 86, 103, 117, 125, 136, 138–42, 147, 150, 154, 157–8, 173, 208, 213, 219
demography xx, 1, 59, 94, 123, 173, 175; British Jewry 65–75, 197–8; demographic pioneers xviii, 65, 192; healthy life expectancy 38; older British Jews 73–5, 88–9; United Kingdom 33–9
Department of Health 15–16, 54–5, 57, 86, 118
Department of Social Security 17
dependency (*see also* structured dependency, independence) 146, 152–3, 160–1, 203, 207, 220
depression 102–3

Developing Services for Black Older People 57
diabetes 102–3, 109, 220
digital divide 217
Directory of Jewish Social Services 215
disabled facilities grant 42
discrimination 151
Dobson, Frank 18
domiciliary care 40–2, 50–1, 59, 76–80, 89, 93, 105–6, 171, 190, 201–3, 207
Donisthorpe Hall 84, 96
drug dependency 103
Dundee 70

eating disorder 103
'edifice complex' 172
Education Act 12
Edward I 25
elder abuse 151
elderly mentally infirm (EMI) 133, 174, 186, 217
Ethics of the Fathers 19
ethnic minorities 57–8, 109, 113, 169, 194; health of 103–4, 220–1

faith-based schooling xx, 75
family and community support structures 197, 219–20
family, role of 20–3, 121, 125, 157, 222
financing services xix–xxi, 15,

17–9, 28, 33, 41–2, 47–51, 53–9, 86, 113–4, 120–1, 130, 165–72, 195, 198–9, 201–2, 222
food (*see also* Jewish-style food, kosher food) 138–44, 151, 153
Ford, Henry 156
Foucault, Michel 149
friendly societies 11
friendship clubs 76, 190
Future Imperfect? 58, 177

Gateshead 76
General Social Care Council 51
gittim (religious divorces) 69
Glasgow 70, 81, 118, 174, 202, 210, 212–13
Glasgow Jewish Housing Association 80
Goffman, Erving 149
Goldberg, Jacqueline xx
Golders Green/Hendon, London 76
Gorbals, Glasgow 196
Governance in the Jewish Voluntary Sector xix, 184
Government Actuary Department 4, 34–7, 191–3
Grant-making Trusts in the Jewish Sector xix
Greengross, Baroness 207
'grey pound' 3

'grey power' 3, 193
guilds 10

Hackney, London borough of 70, 84, 122, 198, 204
halakhah (Jewish law) 19, 67–8, 180
Halfpenny, Peter ix, 183
Hand-in-Hand Asylum for Aged and Decayed Tradesmen 26
Haredi Jews *see* strictly Orthodox Jews
Harris, Margaret xix, 184
Harrow, London borough of 70, 84
Hartrigg Oaks 206
hatzolla (community medical service) 77
heart disease 102–3, 109
Heathlands 84, 123, 170–1, 173, 212
hekdesh (infirmary) 23
Help the Aged 118, 152
Herzl-Moser Jewish Hospital 95
hesed (kindness) 76
hevra kadisha (holy brotherhood) 22, 76
hevrot (brotherhoods) 22
high blood pressure 102–3, 109
Holocaust (*see also* antisemitism, pogroms) 128–9, 145, 181
Home Alone 46

Home and Hospital for Jewish Incurables 26
Home for Aged Jews 95
Home from Home 118
hospices 156
hospital 10–11, 15, 17, 23, 26, 41, 43, 47–8, 57, 76, 79, 95, 110, 116, 135, 201
'hotels-with-care' 14, 124, 137, 159–60, 174
household tasks 38, 47, 104, 109
houses of correction 10
Housing Corporation 44
Housing Grants, Construction and Regeneration Act 42
Hull 94
human resources *see* staffing

incontinence 139–40, 143
independence (*see also* dependency, de-institutionalization) 9, 41, 48, 56–7, 138, 151–3, 156, 158, 161, 203–4, 206, 213
Industrial Dwelling Society 80
informal care 40, 43, 106, 191
information technology (IT) (*see also* computers, websites) 209, 214–19
inspection authorities (*see also* inspection reports) 208
inspection reports (*see also* inspection authorities) 118, 120
institutionalization (*see also* de–institutionalization, dependency) 38, 134, 145–51, 161, 220
intermarriage *see* assimilation
intermediate care 56–7
Investors in People 182
Israel xix, 21

Jerusalem Fellows 182
Jewish Association for the Physically Handicapped (*see also* Jewish Care) 27
Jewish Blind and Disabled 80
Jewish Blind Society (*see also* Jewish Care) 27
Jewish Board of Guardians, Leeds 95
Jewish Care 27–8, 77–9, 81, 118, 128, 173–4, 182–3, 198, 210, 215
Jewish Care Scotland 117, 202
Jewish Chronicle 79, 141
Jewish festivals 25, 99, 126, 148, 181
Jewish Home and Hospital at Tottenham (*see also* Jewish Care) 27
Jewish identity 67
Jewish Poor Board 26
Jewish Soup Kitchen, Manchester 212
Jewish-style food (*see also* food, kosher food) 129, 137, 140, 142, 148

Jewish Welfare Board (*see also* Jewish Care) 27
Jewish.co.uk 216
Jimack, Michael 86–7
Joel Emanuel almshouses 26
Joseph Rowntree Foundation 206

Kansas City 206
King, Imogene 156
King's Fund 58, 118, 177
kosher food (*see also* food, Jewish-style food) 77–9, 87–8, 126–7, 129, 131, 140, 142, 148, 168, 181
Kosmin, Barry xx

Lady Sarah Cohen home (*see also* Jewish Care) 174
Langdon College 212
Langer, Ellen 152–3
League of Jewish Women 77–8, 183
Leeds 81, 93–6, 210, 220, 221
Leeds Jewish Community Study xxi, 5, 93–111, 196; accommodation 107–9; general and income characteristics 97–9; health 102–4; Jewish attitudes and practices 99–102; mobility 104–7
Leeds Jewish Housing Association 80

Leeds Jewish Welfare Board (LJWB) 96
Leylands, Leeds 95
lifetime homes 213
Liverpool 26, 81, 94–5, 210
Liverpool Jewish Housing Association 80
livery companies 10
Logan, Winifred 156
London and the South-east xxi, 10, 25–6, 28, 68, 70, 72, 78–80, 82, 84–8, 108, 117–19, 122–3, 128, 167, 171, 175–6, 196, 198, 200, 204, 210, 215, 217
long-standing illness 38, 86, 102, 109, 214
Long-term Planning for British Jewry xviii–xxi

Maccabi 202
Maimonides 20
mainstreaming 34, 58, 194
Major, John 17
Manchester 70, 78, 81, 95, 123, 173, 175, 210–13, 215
Manchester Jewish Community Care 212
Manchester Jewish Federation 80, 212
Manchester Jewish Housing Association 212
market 17, 160, 165, 174, 195, 199, 206
marriage 23–4, 69

Masorti (Conservative Judaism) 67
meals-on-wheels 4, 75, 78–9, 89, 106, 184, 190, 212
means test 49, 120
mediaeval period 9, 13, 20, 22
mental health needs (*see also* cognitive functioning difficulties, dementia) 221
Microsoft 218
Middle Ages 9
Ministry of Health *see* Department of Health
Ministry of Housing 16
mission drift 202
mitzvot (good deeds) 19
mobile phones 99
models of care 146, 155–6
Modernising Social Services 48
Moortown, Leeds 95
morbidity rate 38
Morris Feinmann 123, 212
Moving into a Care Home 118

National Assistance Act 12, 14–15
National Assistance Board 14
National Care Standards Commission (NCSC) 51
national census 66, 192
National Health Service (NHS) 13, 17, 33, 58, 95, 110, 117
National Health Service Act 12
National Health Service and Community Act 17–18, 114
National Insurance Act 12
National Lottery Charities Board (Scotland) 202
national minimum standards 19, 33, 51, 59–60, 146, 155, 186, 189, 194, 199–200
National Network for Jewish Social Housing 211
National Service Framework for Older People 19, 48, 56
National Survey of British Jewry (*see also* Leeds Jewish Community Study, Long-term Planning for British Jewry) xxi, 93, 96, 109, 122, 196, 219
National Training Organisation (NTO) 52
National Vocational Qualification (NVQ) 52, 182
Netherlands 206
(New) Labour Party/government 1, 12–13, 18, 26, 33, 48–60, 193, 195
Newark Lodge 174
Newcastle 81, 84
Newlands 212
Newport 69
NHS Plan 9, 48, 56

Nightingale House 26, 84, 122–3, 183
North Kent 72, 123
North Surrey 72, 123
Norwood Child Care (*see also* Norwood-Ravenswood) 27
Norwood-Ravenswood 210
Nottingham 81, 84

occupational therapy 42
Office for Standards in Education (OFSTED) 51
Old Age Pension Act 14
Orem, Dorothea 156
Otto Schiff Housing Association (OSHA) (*see also* Jewish Care) 27, 128
Outreach Community and Residential Services 212

Parkinson's disease 103
paternalism 152, 176
pensions 14, 39, 49, 97–9, 110, 113, 172, 197
Personal Social Services Research Unit (PSSRU) 33, 38
physiotherapy 137, 146, 154
pogroms (*see also* antisemitism, Holocaust)) 68, 95
Poor Law 10–11, 14–16, 25, 29, 146, 149, 189, 207
poverty 20, 25–6

Prestwich, Manchester 70, 76
professionalism xx, 176
Progressive Judaism 67, 95, 100
promoting independence grant 57, 201
protectsia (influence) 120

quality assurance (*see also* best value) 209

Race Relations (Amendment) Act 56, 194
rationing, care homes 119
Redbank, Manchester 196
Redbridge, London borough of 70, 84
Registered Homes Act (*see also* Care Standards Act) 51
rehabilitation 57, 146, 154, 200
Reid, Margaret xix, 183
relatives *see* family, role of
religion and spirituality 148, 161
residents' meetings 138, 157–9
respiratory illness (*see also* asthma) 48
retirement 60
Rochester, Colin xix, 184
Roper, Nancy 156
Rosetrees (*see also* Jewish Care) 198
Rowntree 14–15
Roy, Callista 156

Royal Commission on Long Term Care 18–19, 33, 40, 42, 46, 49–50, 54, 167, 193, 218
Royal Commission on the Poor Laws 14
Rucker, Sir Arthur 15

Sabbath 126, 141–2, 148, 180
Sabbath Meals Society 26
Saints of Germany 20
Salford *see* Broughton Park, Manchester
Sanhedrin (Temple court) 21
satisfaction surveys 46, 156–9
Scandinavia 206
Schlesinger, Ernest xix
semi-formal care 76, 191
Sheffield 95
sheltered housing 4, 16, 40, 41, 44–6, 75–6, 80–1, 89, 108–10, 156, 173, 190, 193, 196; obsolescent stock (*see also* very sheltered housing) 45, 204
shtetl (Eastern European small town) 23
Sinclair House (*see also* Jewish Care) 27
smart homes 213
social construction of old age 150
Social Services Inspectorate 57
Social Services Modernisation Fund 58
Soup Kitchen for the Jewish Poor 26–7
soup kitchens 11
South Hertfordshire 72, 85
Southport 81, 84
Spanish and Portuguese Hospital 26
special needs housing 205
staffing 176–7, 200; attitudes of 16, 147; Jewish ethos 147–8; Jewish recruitment and Judaism training 178–83, 210–12; non-Jewish 127, 181; recruitment and retention issues xx, 127, 143, 146, 154, 165, 177–8, 207, 221
stair lifts 42
Stamford Hill, London 76, 126, 179
Statute on Charitable Uses 10–11
Statutory Spending Assessment (SSA) 54, 201
Stephen Lawrence inquiry report 57
Stepney (Bnai Brith) Clubs and Settlement (*see also* Jewish Care) 27
stereotypes 3–4, 194, 215
stimulation 146, 154, 220
strangers, needs of 21
Strangeways, Manchester 196

Strategic Plan (*see also* Long-term Planning for British Jewry) xxi
strictly Orthodox Jews xix, 67, 70, 75–6, 80, 84, 100, 102, 109, 122–3, 126, 179–80, 197, 200, 203–4
'strip-washing' 140
stroke 142, 154
structured dependency 150–1
Supporting People 19, 57, 201
synagogues 25, 67, 69, 76, 88, 95, 99, 126–8, 191, 196, 203

Talmud 19–22
television 126, 135, 144, 154
Thatcher, Margaret 17
The Financial Resources of the Jewish Voluntary Sector xix, 183
The Future of Jewish Schooling in the United Kingdom xx
The Last Refuge 149–50
They Look After Their Own, Don't They? 57
Tierney, Alison 156
Torah 20–2
Torquay 69
Totallyjewish.com 216
Townsend, Peter 15, 149–51
trade clubs 11

Union of Orthodox Synagogues 69

United Jewish Israel Appeal 182
urine, smell of 125, 135
user empowerment/involvement 52, 151–56, 208, 220–1

Valins, Oliver xv, xx
very sheltered housing (*see also* sheltered housing) 44–6
volunteers xx, 22, 26, 43, 75, 89, 99, 134, 144–8, 157, 176, 183–5, 187, 191, 214, 221

waiting lists 119
Walton Community Care Centre 202, 212–13
warden-call systems (*see also* sheltered housing) 204–5
Waverley Manor (*see also* Jewish Care) 27
websites (*see also* computers, information technology) 215–16
weekly costs of institutional care (*see also* financing services) 166–8
Welfare State 9, 12–13, 26–9, 189, 195
Wolfenden Committee 13
workhouse 9–11, 14, 25, 150

York 206

zedakah (charity) 19–20, 22

JPR publications

Planning for Jewish communities

Oliver Valins, Barry Kosmin and Jacqueline Goldberg
The future of Jewish schooling in the United Kingdom: A strategic assessment of a faith-based provision of primary and secondary school education
JPR Report no. 2, 2001

Margaret Harris and Colin Rochester
Governance in the Jewish voluntary sector
JPR Report no. 1, 2001

Peter Halfpenny and Margaret Reid
The financial resources of the UK Jewish voluntary sector
JPR Report no. 1, 2000

Ernest Schlesinger
Grant-making trusts in the Jewish sector
JPR Report no. 2, 2000

Barry A. Kosmin, Jacqueline Goldberg, Milton Shain and Shirley Bruk
Jews of the 'new South Africa': highlights of the 1998 national survey of South African Jews
JPR Report no. 3, September 1999

Barry A. Kosmin and Jacqueline Goldberg
Patterns of charitable giving among British Jews
JPR Report no. 2, July 1998

Jacqueline Goldberg and Barry A. Kosmin
The social attitudes of unmarried young Jews in contemporary Britain
JPR Report no. 4, June 1997

Margaret Harris
The Jewish voluntary sector in the United Kingdom: its role and its future
JPR Policy Paper no. 5, May 1997

Stephen Miller, Marlena Schmool and Antony Lerman
Social and political attitudes of British Jews: some key findings of the JPR survey
JPR Report no. 1, February 1996

Jewish culture: arts, media, heritage

JPR Working Party on Television
A guide to Jewish television: prospects and possibilities: findings of the Working Party
JPR Policy Paper no. 3, July 1999

David Clark
Developing Jewish museums in Europe
JPR Report no. 1, February 1999

Stanley Waterman
Cultural politics and European Jewry
JPR Policy Paper no. 1, February 1999

Roger Silverstone
Jewish television: prospects and possibilities
JPR Policy paper no. 1, March 1998

Civil society

Paul Iganski (ed.)
The hate debate: Should hate be punished as a crime?
Published in association with Profile Books, London

Antisemitism and Xenophobia Today
published electronically by JPR
Web address: www.axt.org.uk

Patterns of Prejudice
a JPR quarterly journal in association with the Parkes Centre of the University of Southampton, and published (print and on-line) by Sage Publications

JPR Law Panel
Combating Holocaust denial through law in the United Kingdom: report of the panel
JPR Report no. 3, 2000

Barry A. Kosmin
Ethnic and religious questions in the 2001 UK Census of Population: policy recommendations
JPR Policy Paper no. 2, March 1999

Margaret Brearley
The Roma/Gypsies of Europe: a persecuted people
JPR Policy Paper no. 3, December 1996

David Capitanchik and Michael Whine
The governance of cyberspace: racism on the Internet
JPR Policy Paper no. 2, July 1996

Diana Pinto
A new Jewish identity for post-1989 Europe
JPR Policy Paper no. 1, June 1996

Israel: impact, society, identity

Ariela Keysar and Barry A. Kosmin
North American Conservative Jewish teenagers' attachment to Israel
JPR Report no. 2, July 1999

Steven Kaplan and Hagar Salamon
Ethiopian immigrants in Israel: experience and prospects
JPR Report no. 1, March 1998

Barry A. Kosmin, Antony Lerman and Jacqueline Goldberg
The attachment of British Jews to Israel
JPR Report no. 5, November 1997

Other publications

Commission on Representation of the Interests of the British Jewish Community
A Community of Communities: Report of the Commission
March 2000

www.jpr.org.uk

Available on the website are *JPR News* and recent JPR reports

To order copies of JPR publications, please contact:
Institute for Jewish Policy Research
79 Wimpole Street
London W1G 9RY
tel +44 (0)20 7935 8266 fax +44 (0)20 7935 3252
e-mail jpr@jpr.org.uk